Q   446796
635   21.27
Sum   Oct88
Summer vegetables

DATE DUE			
604-CC	cmle March 10, 2000 IU		
12-12-97			
cmle Feb 23 98 IU			(4042)
cmle Oct 9 98 IU			
510			3020
10-9-98			770-00
cmle Mar 1 99 IU			
3414			
3-1-99			
cmle Oct 7 99 IU			
421			
10-7-99			

604-C

The Time-Life Gardener's Guide

SUMMER VEGETABLES

A

BOOK

Other Publications:

MYSTERIES OF THE UNKNOWN
TIME FRAME
FIX IT YOURSELF
FITNESS, HEALTH & NUTRITION
SUCCESSFUL PARENTING
HEALTHY HOME COOKING
UNDERSTANDING COMPUTERS
LIBRARY OF NATIONS
THE ENCHANTED WORLD
THE KODAK LIBRARY OF CREATIVE PHOTOGRAPHY
GREAT MEALS IN MINUTES
THE CIVIL WAR
PLANET EARTH
COLLECTOR'S LIBRARY OF THE CIVIL WAR
THE EPIC OF FLIGHT
THE GOOD COOK
WORLD WAR II
HOME REPAIR AND IMPROVEMENT
THE OLD WEST

For information on and a full description of any of
the Time-Life Books series listed above, please call 1-800-621-7026
or write:

Reader Information
Time-Life Customer Service
P.O. Box C-32068
Richmond, Virginia 23261-2068

This book is one of a series of guides to good gardening.

The Time-Life Gardener's Guide

SUMMER VEGETABLES

TIME-LIFE BOOKS, ALEXANDRIA, VIRGINIA

52 0296

CONTENTS

1
LAYING THE GROUNDWORK

2
MAKING THINGS GROW

3
TENDING YOUR GARDEN

Probably because mankind has been systematically cultivating vegetables for at least 5,000 years, most people retain a deep urge to produce at least some of their own foodstuffs. Watching squashes grow plump and tomatoes turn red is exciting in itself, and holds the promise of wonderful eating to come. Vegetables brought straight from garden plot to kitchen pot taste better than the store-bought varieties; further, their vitamin and mineral content is at its peak.

This volume tells how, with even just a small patch of sunny outdoor space, you can have those satisfactions. The first section explains how to do the groundwork of planning a plot and digging the soil. The second shows in detail the best ways to plant crops so they will continue producing through the growing season. The third covers maintenance, with special attention to those enduring favorites, corn and tomatoes; and the fourth illustrates the varied methods of harvesting different crops.

Following these is a section of special techniques used by experts and a map of spring frost dates. Finally, there is an illustrated dictionary that describes more than 40 kinds of vegetables, and tells where and how they prosper best.

<table>
<tr><td>4</td><td>5</td><td>6</td></tr>
</table>

HARVESTING YOUR CROPS

MAKING THE MOST OF NATURE

DICTIONARY OF VEGETABLES

1
LAYING
THE GROUNDWORK

From the first crisp carrots of early summer to the last sweet squash of fall, a vegetable garden is a constantly changing delight. There is the pleasure of anticipation, of watching as beets and carrots shoulder their way into view, as beans swell in their pods, cucumbers lengthen and corn puts out silky tassels. Then there is the enjoyment of consuming the harvest, fresh-picked and full of flavor.

But good vegetable gardens never arrive at this perfection unassisted. They produce bumper crops because someone has paid attention to the important preliminaries: to siting and soil preparation. To be succulent, vegetables need sun, preferably throughout the day, and they need a friable, well-drained soil rich in the nutrients that promote healthy growth.

On the following pages you will find information that will help you create a bountiful vegetable garden. How to plot the changing patterns of light and shade throughout the growing season. How to cultivate the soil so that it encourages well-developed roots—the underpinnings of sturdy plants and, in the case of root crops such as radishes and carrots, the vegetable itself. How to build your own compost pile to use for soil conditioner. How to understand the mysteries of pH, along with formulas for correcting the pH balance of your soil. How to test your soil for the three essential nutrients—potassium for sturdy stems, nitrogen for luxuriant leaves and phosphorus for strong roots. Finally, because you will be using tools all summer long to keep down the weeds and aerate the soil, there is a section on how to select and care for such classic garden hand tools as spades, rakes and hoes.

STARTING
A VEGETABLE PLOT

Wherever you live, you can grow vegetables. Whether your climate is warm or cold, your terrain hilly or flat, your property large or small, you can have the satisfactions of raising and eating your own fresh vegetables.

The first requirement is forethought. To begin, select the site with care. The vegetable garden as a whole must be located where it will have sunlight—at least for seven hours of the day. Within the garden, the placement of specific vegetables is important, too; a few vegetables need the cooling relief of part-time shade *(pages 52-53)*.

Vegetables need protection from other elements as well. If possible, the garden should be placed on the sheltered side of a hedge or a row of trees that can serve as a windbreak, because strong winds can uproot tender seedlings and blow down crops that are top-heavy when ripe. Wind can also dry out soil, and vegetables need plenty of moisture. But vegetables also need well-drained soil, so don't put the garden at the foot of a hill—or any other spot where too much water is apt to collect.

Next, consider the space requirements. Asparagus needs 18 inches between plants and 36 inches between rows; beans need only 6 inches between plants and 24 inches between rows—and yield more vegetables per plant besides. Seed packet instructions generally use a 15-foot row as a measure for determining yield. From that you can judge how much space to devote to vegetables and which ones you have room to grow.

When you have selected the site and the size for your garden, you are ready to prepare the ground for planting. The best time to do so is when the soil is soft—some time after the last spring frost in your area *(pages 80-81)*. Pick up a handful of soil, make a ball and drop it. If it falls apart, the soil is workable; if it sticks together, it is too hard or too wet. Once you have determined that the soil can be worked, follow some basic steps *(right and opposite)* for laying out the bed, tilling the soil and marking the placement of your vegetable rows.

Neat rows of beans, leaf vegetables and root crops soak up sunlight in a garden bordered with eye-pleasing iris and peonies. Wide paths between rows allow for easy fertilizing, weeding and—the reason for it all—harvesting.

1 Mark the perimeter of your vegetable garden with stakes and string. Facing into the garden, dig down with a spade just inside the marked perimeter to the depth of the blade; then turn the sod over into the garden area *(below)*. Repeat all along the perimeter. Remove the stakes and string for easy access.

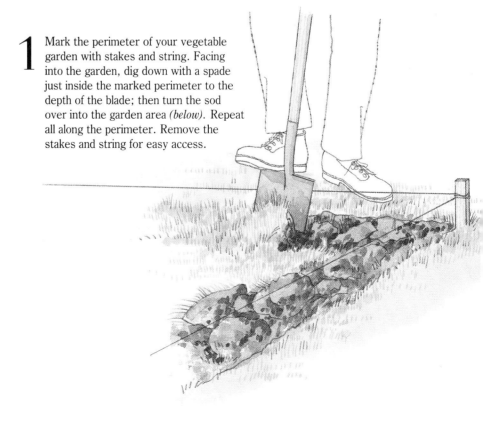

2 Using a spade, turn over all the sod within the marked boundaries. Break up any compacted clods. To make sure that you don't leave patches of unturned soil, work in rows, completing one row before moving on to the next.

3 Till the entire area with a rotary tiller *(right)* to the depth of one tiller blade —approximately 8 to 10 inches. Add organic matter—and, if needed, lime and fertilizer *(pages 10-17)*—and till under. Remove large stones. Rake the area smooth.

4 After you have amended the soil and decided what you want to plant, stake out rows for vegetables and mark each row with string. Follow seed packet directions for spacing between rows. Use plastic labels or attach the names of varieties to wooden tongue depressors; they will serve as guides for planting now and help you identify your crops later as they sprout. □

YOUR SOIL AND ITS pH—
AN ACID TEST

Rows of lettuce and Chinese cabbage grow fat and leafy in a neatly tended garden. The soil's pH can be maintained at a level congenial to vegetables by periodic applications of lime (to correct acidity) or sulfur (if the soil is too alkaline).

Among the most important factors in vegetable gardening is the pH level of the soil. The term "pH" represents a measurement of the soil's acidity or alkalinity on a scale of 0 to 14. The number 7 represents neutrality; the lower the number below that, the more acidic the soil is, and the higher the number, the more alkaline it is. Most vegetables prefer a slightly acidic soil, one having a pH of about 6.5. Soil that is too alkaline does not promote the chemical activity required for attracting the nutrients vegetables need to grow. Soil that is too acidic attracts nutrients, but then will not release them. But excess acidity can be corrected by adding lime to the soil, and excess alkalinity by adding sulfur.

In general, areas with clayey soil and high rainfall tend to be acidic; areas with sandy soil and low rainfall have a high salt content, which makes them alkaline. To determine the pH of your soil, gather a sample and test it—either with a do-it-yourself kit of the sort available at garden supply centers and through mail-order suppliers, or by having the test done by your state agricultural extension service, which will do the job for a nominal fee.

Gather the soil sample when the ground is moist but not wet. Dig down 4 to 5 inches with a trowel, remove a scoop of soil and put it in a clean bucket. Repeat in several places around the garden. Mix the scoopfuls together, remove a cupful, seal it in a plastic bag and mail it to the extension service. The test results will tell you not only the pH ratio, but whether you need to add lime or sulfur, and what amounts of either are needed. You can spread them by hand, but for best results, use a drop spreader *(opposite)*.

1 After turning over the soil and calculating how much lime or sulfur you need to add (based on pH test results, soil type and the size of your garden), set the calibration device *(inset)* on the drop spreader. Some spreaders come with recommended settings; if yours does not, set it at the medium opening. Open and close the hopper to make sure the mechanism works. Fill the hopper with lime or sulfur.

2 Walk the spreader around the perimeter of the garden, then up and down in rows. Don't let rows of lime (or sulfur, if that is what you are adding) overlap, or you will overcorrect the problem. Keep the hopper closed on turns between rows. If any lime (or sulfur) is left over, it means your calibration was off. Reset the calibration to a small opening and walk the entire site again so you will have given the garden its full measure of lime or sulfur. Then till it into the soil. □

NUTRIENTS
FOR HEALTHY SOIL

L ike growing children, growing vegetables need a balanced diet. Most soils lack sufficient nutrients to keep vegetables healthy. To find out what's missing and what supplements to add, gather a soil sample *(page 10)* and have it tested by your state agricultural extension service. Or purchase a home-testing kit and do it yourself. Since soil conditions change over time, retest every three to four years.

The three most important nutrients for vegetables are nitrogen (for healthy leaves), phosphorus (for healthy roots) and potassium (for strong stalks and resistance to disease). The test results will tell you exactly how much of these nutrients to add to the soil before planting.

Commercial fertilizers that are sold as "complete" contain all three major nutrients in a predetermined ratio; for example, the numbers 5-10-5 on a label refer to the percentages of nitrogen, phosphorus and potassium in the product. Follow the manufacturer's instructions for application. Too much of any nutrient can be as harmful to plants as too little. Organic fertilizers such as animal manure, fish meal and alfalfa meal are also good sources of nutrients. If possible, use aged, dry manure; unless it is plowed into the soil in the fall and allowed to decompose over the winter, fresh manure can injure roots; it also begets weeds that will compete with the crops.

There are several alternative methods of applying fertilizer. One is to spread fertilizer evenly over the site with a drop spreader and then turn the soil under to a depth of 3 to 4 inches; for the best results, this should be done in the fall. Another is to fertilize row by row just before spring planting *(opposite)*.

A third method is called side-dressing—placing fertilizer alongside rows—and a variation of that is band-dressing, placing fertilizer in a ring around an individual plant *(box, opposite)*. One or the other of these two methods should be done when plants blossom, and again at three- to four-week intervals until harvest time.

Celery grows crisp and green in soil that has been well fertilized with nitrogen, phosphorus and potassium.

1 To concentrate fertilizer under a seed row before planting, dig a trench along the marked row with a mattock or a hoe *(left)*. The trench should be 2 inches deeper than the recommended depth of the seeds you will plant. This will vary from crop to crop; follow the instructions on the seed packet.

2 Spread 2 to 3 pounds of complete fertilizer (one containing nitrogen, phosophorus and potassium in a ratio such as 5-10-5) into every 100 feet of trench. Use a rake *(below)* to cover the fertilizer with 2 inches of soil. Tamp down. Sow the seeds on top of the soil and cover them with more soil according to instructions on the packet.

3 Once your plants have blossomed, fertilize them again, applying a side-dressing row by row. Use a mattock or a hoe to dig a 2-inch-deep trench alongside each row at the drip line (the outermost edge of the foliage). By hand, spread 2 to 3 pounds of complete fertilizer per 100 feet of trench. Cover with 2 inches of soil. Tamp down. ☐

FERTILIZING PLANT BY PLANT

Instead of side-dressing an entire row, you can band-dress individual plants. With a trowel, dig a trench 2 inches deep around a plant at the drip line. Sprinkle approximately 2 tablespoons of complete fertilizer inside the trench; then refill it with soil.

COMPOST:
NATURE'S SOIL CONDITIONER

Layers of organic matter—leaves, twigs and vegetable refuse—alternate with layers of soil and bone meal in a well-ventilated wooden bin, decomposing into compost that will be used to enrich the garden soil.

After the application of fertilizers, what a vegetable garden needs most is large amounts of the matchless soil-enriching substance called compost. Made of decaying vegetable matter, it is a rich source of natural plant-growing nutrients. Even thin, sandy soil and clayey soil can be made to yield excellent crops if enough compost is worked in before planting. Spread on top of an already growing garden plot, compost makes the best of all possible mulches.

Fortunately, generous supplies of compost can easily be made at home—and with minimal expense. Just establish a compost heap in some out-of-the-way corner of the backyard. Onto the heap go all manner of garden wastes: weeds, leaves, grass clippings, hay, straw and the unused parts of vegetables, such as carrot tops. Also eligible are kitchen scraps—spoiled lettuce, coffee grounds, eggshells, chopped-up corncobs. Meat scraps are not recommended, however, nor are leftover dairy products; they turn rancid and attract rodents. Also avoid clippings from plants sprayed with strong pesticides and weeds heavily freighted with seeds that promise to sprout.

The vegetable refuse goes on the heap in layers, which alternate with other, thinner layers of earth and nitrogen-rich compounds like bone meal. The nitrogen is essential; it feeds the bacteria that help break down the organic wastes into compost. The pile itself can be freestanding, or it can be contained in barrels or bins *(page 17)*. In either case, because the organic breakdown in a well-made compost pile is so thorough, the pile will be odorless—and the compost itself will be clean, crumbly, easy to use, and free of both insects and diseases.

Compost is such an excellent soil conditioner that it would be difficult to use too much. As a rule of thumb when turning over a garden plot, mix in one-third as much compost as there is earth. That is, if spading the soil to a depth of, say, 9 inches, work in a 3-inch layer of good, rich compost.

1 Having chosen a secluded location for your compost heap, break up the soil that will be underneath the pile with a garden fork. This will promote drainage from the bottom of the pile. The area should be about 3 feet square, but no more than 5 feet square.

2 Again using a garden fork, spread a 4-inch layer of organic matter—fallen leaves, twigs and branches, old vegetable stalks, kitchen scraps—on top of the broken-up soil.

3 After putting down the first layer of organic matter, sprinkle on a thin layer of bone meal, fish meal, blood meal or other substance containing nitrogen. Then spade on a thin stratum of ordinary soil. This done, make a second layer of organic matter 4 or 5 inches thick, repeat the application of nitrogenous material and earth—and so on. A finished compost heap should be about 3 feet high.

4 When a few layers have been built up, wet the pile with a hose. Moisture helps activate the bacteria in the heap, and also helps create heat—which speeds the process of decomposition, kills weeds and generally purifies the entire pile. If there is little rain, water the heap weekly, and turn over the layers each week with a fork to distribute the moisture and keep the compost aerated. To conserve both moisture and warmth, you can cover the pile with an old blanket or rug, or with a sheet of black plastic. □

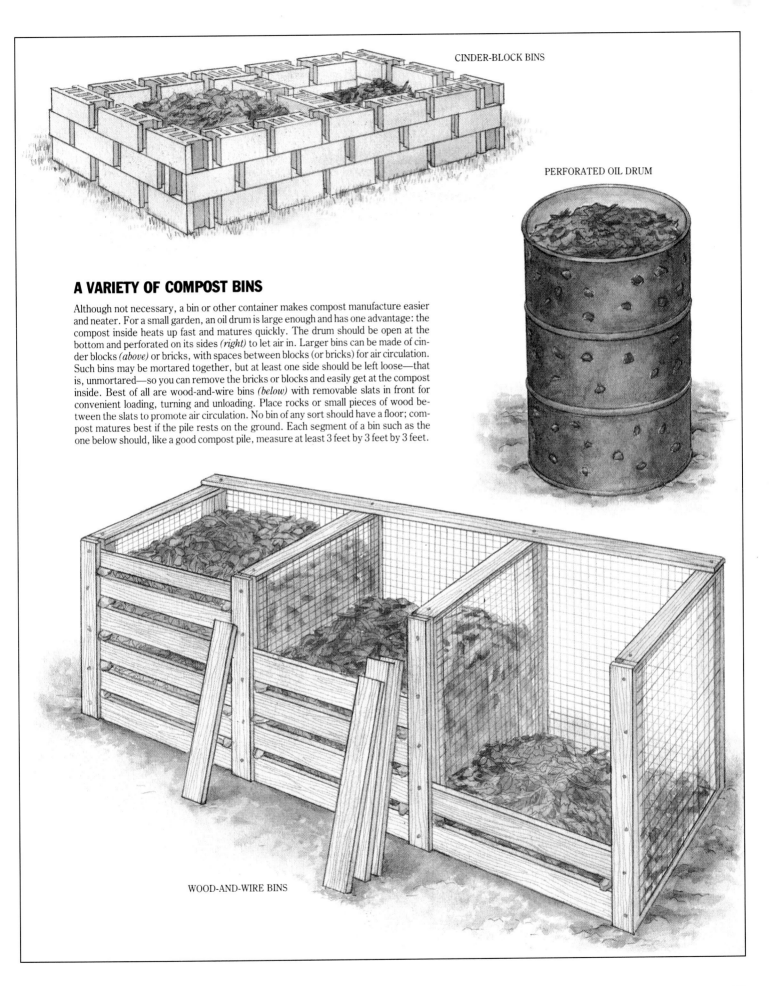

CINDER-BLOCK BINS

PERFORATED OIL DRUM

A VARIETY OF COMPOST BINS

Although not necessary, a bin or other container makes compost manufacture easier and neater. For a small garden, an oil drum is large enough and has one advantage: the compost inside heats up fast and matures quickly. The drum should be open at the bottom and perforated on its sides *(right)* to let air in. Larger bins can be made of cinder blocks *(above)* or bricks, with spaces between blocks (or bricks) for air circulation. Such bins may be mortared together, but at least one side should be left loose—that is, unmortared—so you can remove the bricks or blocks and easily get at the compost inside. Best of all are wood-and-wire bins *(below)* with removable slats in front for convenient loading, turning and unloading. Place rocks or small pieces of wood between the slats to promote air circulation. No bin of any sort should have a floor; compost matures best if the pile rests on the ground. Each segment of a bin such as the one below should, like a good compost pile, measure at least 3 feet by 3 feet by 3 feet.

WOOD-AND-WIRE BINS

SITING A GARDEN
TO MAKE THE MOST OF THE SUN

Plants need sunlight, even more than compost and fertilizer, to grow. Most need at least seven hours of it each sunny day, or they may be stunted. So a vegetable garden should ideally be placed in full sun, and planted in such a fashion that the sunlight does the most good.

This is not always easy to achieve, especially in restricted backyard plots. Houses, walls and trees cast shadows that can be tricky to calculate. For example, in northern latitudes shadows stretch longer in all seasons than they do in, say, the Middle Atlantic states or the Deep South because of the sun's lower angle. For the same reason, shadows grow longer in all regions during the early spring and the autumn than they do during the bright days of June and July.

When siting a vegetable plot, therefore, take into account the sun's angle at various seasons and figure out in advance where plant-stunting shadows will fall. A wall that looks innocent in the brightness of May may throw part of a plot into deep shadow by late summer. Especially avoid a site where an obstruction will block the sun during the hot noonday hours when sunlight does vegetables the most good. The best strategy, then, is to locate a garden as far from obstructions as possible, and to try to angle the plot so that it faces south—toward the sun—with any walls or trees on its northern border.

This is good advice in fact for siting any garden, even one in an ideal open area with no trees or walls anywhere about. A plot angled north-south, as in the example on the opposite page, gives all the vegetables an equal share in the straight-on rays of the noonday sun, and the canted light of morning and afternoon as well, as the sun moves in its diurnal round from east to west.

Some shading by one plant of another is all right. If your garden is shaded part of the time, remember that leafy vegetables like lettuce and spinach, and the root vegetables, can get by with less than a full day's sun. But daylong sunshine is a necessity for plants that throw extra energy into producing fruit, such as tomatoes, squash and peppers.

Tall-growing cornstalks shade a row of lettuce plants from the sharply slanted beams of an afternoon sun. In midsummer, lettuce needs partial shade during a portion of each day.

HOW THE SHADOWS FALL

The drawing at right shows the pattern of light and shade in an imaginary, but ideal, garden located at 40° north latitude—that is, along the line that runs more or less through New York, Indianapolis, Topeka and Denver to Sacramento. The garden is oriented north *(top)* to south, with the rows running east-west to catch the full benefit of the sun. The time is 10 a.m., as the west-leaning shadows indicate. The vegetables are planted so that they do not shade one another. The tallest, corn, is at the north end of the plot; the shortest, lettuce, is at the southern end. □

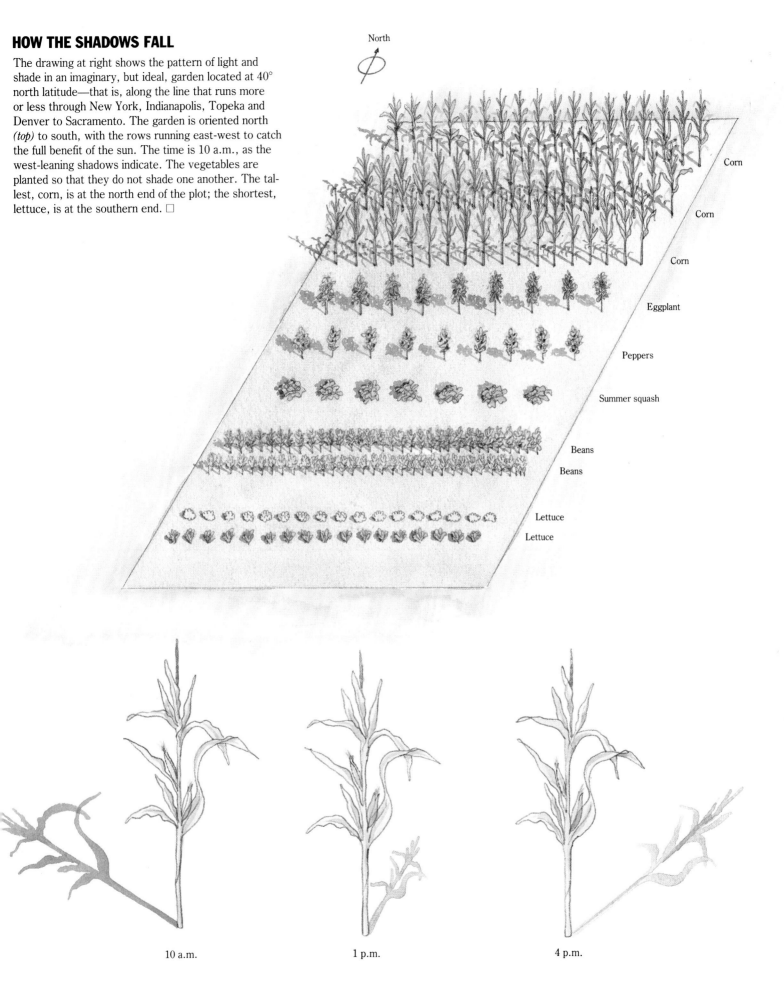

North

Corn

Corn

Corn

Eggplant

Peppers

Summer squash

Beans

Beans

Lettuce

Lettuce

10 a.m.

1 p.m.

4 p.m.

TAKING CARE
OF YOUR GARDEN TOOLS

Three principal tools are needed for vegetable gardening: a spade, a hoe and a rake. The classic garden spade—the short-handled and flat-bladed sort—is especially useful for slicing sod and edging a plot as well as for digging. But it is a good idea to have a long-handled shovel as well, for scooping up loose materials such as sand and topsoil.

It is also helpful to have at least two different hoes, one with a flat working edge to break up surface soil and remove weeds, the other with a narrow, pointed blade; the latter is useful for making narrow trenches for planting seeds and for weeding between rows.

Only one rake is needed for vegetable gardens, but it must be of a particular sort—a garden rake, the kind with short teeth and a compact forged steel head. Fan-shaped leaf rakes are too flexible and light for leveling and cleaning garden beds.

Another useful implement is a heavy-duty spading fork for turning over sod, loosening earth, chopping up clods and digging up root crops when they are ready to harvest. The sort with square tines is best; it is less likely to bend than a fork with rectangular tines.

Among other useful tools are a hand fork and a trowel for planting, a wheelbarrow or a garden cart for moving soil and harvested crops, and a long hose for watering. Finally, a tool used by farmers since time immemorial: the mattock. With its heavy 10-inch head, a pick on one end and a hoelike blade on the other, it will break up hardened earth faster than any other hand implement known.

Hoes and other garden tools should have sharp cutting edges; a dull hoe is a nuisance. How to keep one clean and sharp is shown below and on the opposite page.

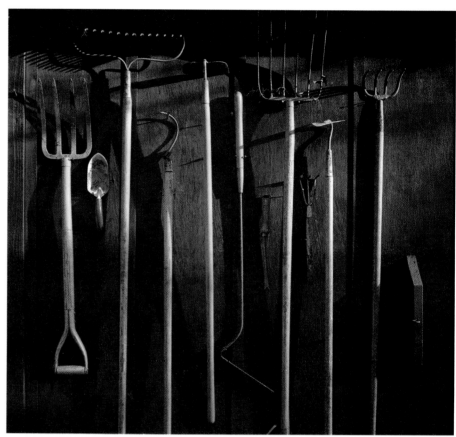

Well-kept garden forks, rakes and weeders hang neatly on a barn wall. Top-quality tools with tempered steel heads and smooth, sturdy ashwood handles are the best.

1 Before sharpening your hoe, scrape any accumulated dirt off the blade with a wire brush. This treatment is also good for spades, shovels, the tines of garden forks and all other garden implements; it will add years of use by discouraging rust. Storing tools in a dry place is essential.

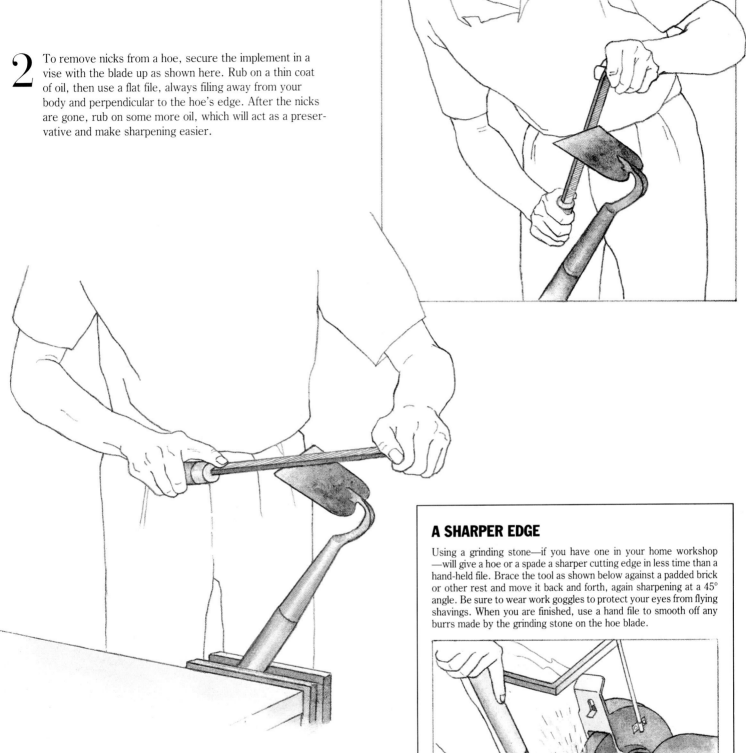

2 To remove nicks from a hoe, secure the implement in a vise with the blade up as shown here. Rub on a thin coat of oil, then use a flat file, always filing away from your body and perpendicular to the hoe's edge. After the nicks are gone, rub on some more oil, which will act as a preservative and make sharpening easier.

3 To sharpen the blade, hold a flat file at a 45° angle, and drive it down and away (not back and forth) in separate motions as you traverse the cutting edge. □

A SHARPER EDGE

Using a grinding stone—if you have one in your home workshop —will give a hoe or a spade a sharper cutting edge in less time than a hand-held file. Brace the tool as shown below against a padded brick or other rest and move it back and forth, again sharpening at a 45° angle. Be sure to wear work goggles to protect your eyes from flying shavings. When you are finished, use a hand file to smooth off any burrs made by the grinding stone on the hoe blade.

2
MAKING THINGS GROW

Like all living things, vegetables benefit from tender loving care when young. Given a good send-off, they are much more likely to mature into healthy, heavy-bearing plants. Nature of course plays a critical role, providing the warm sun and gentle rain that encourage seeds to sprout and young seedlings to develop strong roots. But human intervention can abet the process in a surprising number of ways. Seeds can be encouraged to germinate, for instance, by being planted when soil conditions are at their optimum—warm enough, moist enough and sufficiently friable to give the emerging sprouts the best of all possible environments. For an extra boost, the seeds can even be started indoors in a minigreenhouse and a sterile growing medium that eliminates many of the bacterial dangers that plague young plants. And when the seedlings emerge, whether grown indoors or out, a variety of thinning and transplanting techniques improve the seedlings' chances enormously by minimizing shock and stress to their tender roots.

In other ways, too, vegetables profit from early attention to their needs. Upright supports can increase yield, for example. One typical support, easily installed and disassembled, is the tepee trellis shown on pages 36-37. Crop yields can also be improved by staggering a particular vegetable's planting dates, and by pairing, in a single row, two compatible vegetables with different maturing dates. In the 70 to 90 days it takes head lettuce to mature, for example, green peppers will be germinating; and when the lettuce has been harvested the slower-growing peppers will be just approaching maturity and able to spread out in the space vacated by the lettuce. Crop rotation, too, can improve vegetable quality by varying the demands made on the soil by different plants.

Information on all these measures for getting plants off to a good start can be found in the pages ahead. Along with them are sections dealing with two subjects related to planting procedures: one explains how to build a raised bed when the existing soil is unfit for use or (in the case of city terraces) nonexistent. The other explains how to start young potato plants, which grow not from seed but from the sprouting eyes of actual potatoes.

SOWING SEEDS INDOORS AHEAD OF THE SEASON

There is no need to resist those nearly irresistible seed catalogs that arrive in late winter, or to stifle the yen to grow things before spring arrives. Many vegetables can be started from seed in the house even while the last snow flurries swirl outside. Starting vegetables from seed has several advantages. Seedlings grown indoors are not at the mercy of birds, insects or heavy spring rains. Seeds cost pennies compared with the dollars needed to purchase trays of nursery-grown seedlings. And a greater variety of vegetables is available in seed form than as started seedlings.

Planting seeds indoors gets a jump on the season. In cold climates where spring comes late and summer is short, plants started indoors can go into the garden soil as soon as it warms, then have time to mature and produce a crop before the first fall frost.

Rushing into the season too eagerly, however, should be avoided. Seedlings that grow indoors too long before transplanting become weak and spindly. To get the timing right, consult the seed packets, which say when their contents can safely be planted outdoors. Then count back the number of weeks—usually six to eight—it takes the seedlings to mature for transplanting.

The main necessities for starting seeds in the house are shallow containers, a sterile planting medium and a source of light. Metal cake tins punched with drainage holes make good planters, as do wooden flats, plastic trays, and pots and pellets made of peat *(box, opposite)*. The medium can be any loose, sterile, weed-free soil mix or the kind of soilless, sometimes premoistened mixture sold at garden centers. Such a mixture, because it is very light, allows the seedlings to pop up through it easily. The last necessity is a sunny window or fluorescent lamps, so the seeds can receive plenty of light once they sprout.

Crisp-looking baby lettuces, started from seed, thrive in a plastic tray filled with planting soil. Two weeks after sowing, the seedlings are about ½ inch high.

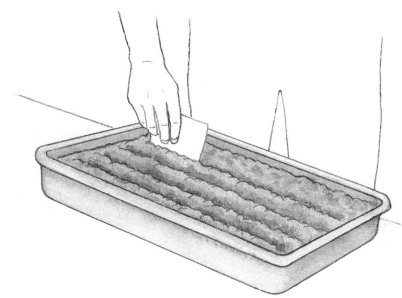

1 Fill a tray with premoistened planting mixture and smooth the surface. Use the edge of a seed packet to make furrows about an inch apart and roughly three times as deep as the diameter of the seeds that you are planting.

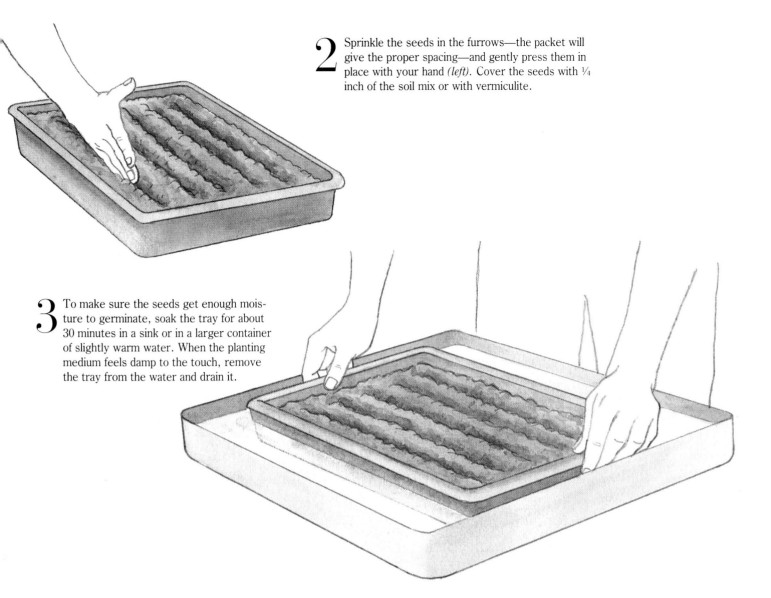

2 Sprinkle the seeds in the furrows—the packet will give the proper spacing—and gently press them in place with your hand *(left)*. Cover the seeds with ¼ inch of the soil mix or with vermiculite.

3 To make sure the seeds get enough moisture to germinate, soak the tray for about 30 minutes in a sink or in a larger container of slightly warm water. When the planting medium feels damp to the touch, remove the tray from the water and drain it.

4 Turn your tray into a minigreenhouse by covering it with a sheet of plastic wrap. Put the tray in a warm place, about 70° F, out of direct sunlight. When the seeds sprout, remove the plastic sheet and move the tray into a location that has full light. □

AN ALTERNATIVE METHOD

With vegetables such as root crops, which do not transplant well, you can start seeds in pellets made of peat instead of using a soil mix. First soak the pellets in water. Press two or three seeds into each pellet; then put the pellets in a tray containing 1 inch of water. Check daily to make sure there is water in the tray. When the seeds sprout, keep the strongest and snip the others. Then transplant the seedlings outdoors, pellets and all.

TRANSPLANTING SEEDLINGS TO GIVE THEM BREATHING SPACE

Given generous amounts of light and moisture, seeds started indoors produce regiments of brisk, green-topped little plants with astonishing swiftness. The trouble is, as the seedlings continue to grow their ranks become overcrowded. At this point thinning is in order, and some transplanting into larger containers to give roots and leaves adequate space for further growth. Without this first indoor move, such plants as tomatoes, lettuce, asparagus and eggplant may not be strong enough to survive the later shift into the garden.

The seedlings are large enough to transplant when they have grown a second pair of leaves. The first step is to collect a supply of containers: peat pots, as shown here, will do fine. So will clay pots, cell packs or even cutoff milk cartons and tin cans. Then purchase some commercial potting soil, which is sterile and loose enough for the delicate roots to grow in.

These supplies at hand, water the seedlings about to be transplanted. Moist soil will cling to the roots and protect them. For seedlings in flat trays, gently lift the plants with a small, flat tool such as a plastic knife, a wooden tongue depressor or a plastic strip of the sort garden centers use as markers. For seedlings in pots, use one hand to scoop up a few at a time *(below)*. Replant the seedlings quickly so that their roots do not dry out. After a short period of additional growth, they will be ready to go outside *(pages 30-31)* or they can mature in a cold frame *(opposite, bottom)*.

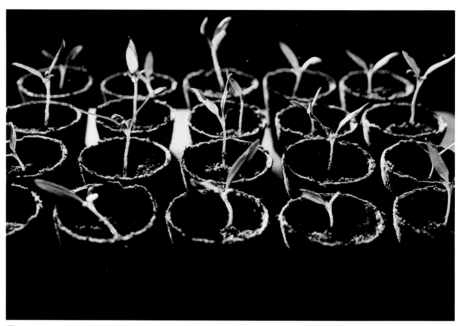

Three-week-old tomato seedlings reach toward the light from peat pots. Started in a flat, they have been transplanted to allow more growing room.

1 To begin transplanting, reach into the pot in which the seeds were sown and lift out a clump of seedlings on the palm of your hand. Be sure you don't pull up the stems, but get all the roots—and the soil around and underneath them as well.

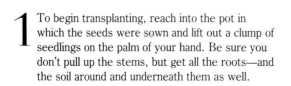

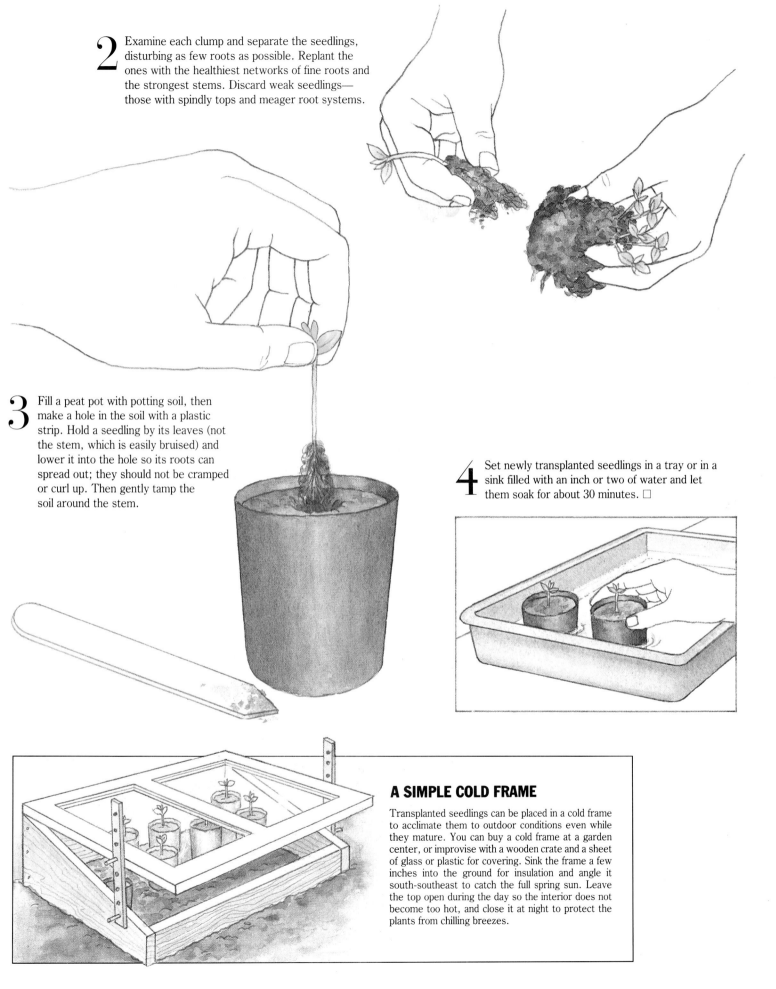

2 Examine each clump and separate the seedlings, disturbing as few roots as possible. Replant the ones with the healthiest networks of fine roots and the strongest stems. Discard weak seedlings—those with spindly tops and meager root systems.

3 Fill a peat pot with potting soil, then make a hole in the soil with a plastic strip. Hold a seedling by its leaves (not the stem, which is easily bruised) and lower it into the hole so its roots can spread out; they should not be cramped or curl up. Then gently tamp the soil around the stem.

4 Set newly transplanted seedlings in a tray or in a sink filled with an inch or two of water and let them soak for about 30 minutes. □

A SIMPLE COLD FRAME

Transplanted seedlings can be placed in a cold frame to acclimate them to outdoor conditions even while they mature. You can buy a cold frame at a garden center, or improvise with a wooden crate and a sheet of glass or plastic for covering. Sink the frame a few inches into the ground for insulation and angle it south-southeast to catch the full spring sun. Leave the top open during the day so the interior does not become too hot, and close it at night to protect the plants from chilling breezes.

CROP ROTATION—A DEFENSE AGAINST PESTS AND DISEASES

The phrase "crop rotation" brings to mind huge fields of wheat and corn stretching across the Kansas plains. But rotating crops, long known to be essential for good yields on large-scale farms, pays off even in relatively small vegetable gardens. It is a good idea before planting seedlings outdoors *(pages 30-31)* to map out a rotation scheme that will be useful in the coming years.

First of all, rotating crops yearly from one part of a garden to another helps control insect pests and the plant diseases they carry. It works because most pests are attracted to only one family of plants. For example, hornworms, whiteflies and Colorado potato beetles zero in solely on members of the potato family (which includes eggplant, peppers and tomatoes). These pests and those that attack other vegetables live in the soil through the winter and attack again the next spring. But if the crops they feed on are moved next season, the pests will be left behind and die for want of food and the vacated plot will be safe for plants of another family.

Crop rotation also avoids depleting the soil of nutrients. Some plants soak up nutrients at a ferocious rate, among them such favorites as broccoli and corn. Others, including most root crops, are not as greedy. So it is best to rotate heavy feeders, not planting them in the same area two years running. Similarly, leafy vegetables consume lots of nitrogen, and root crops need large amounts of potassium. It is beneficial to plant, say, a leafy lettuce where beets were grown last year rather than another root crop, like carrots.

The sample plan on the opposite page shows how a garden can be divided into several plots for rotating purposes, and how they might be planted to minimize both soil depletion and the depredations of crop-ruining pests and diseases. The arrangement does not have to be a rectangle, and if you have room enough the plots can be as far apart as you like. But you will need at least 2 feet between plots to keep the pests at a safe distance. A paving of brick or cinder blocks is not necessary, but makes walking easy for weeding and watering and harvesting.

Healthy, pest-free lettuce, beet greens and carrots share space in a thriving garden. Carrots and beets attract the same pests and should be rotated into a new bed each year. Lettuce and other leaf crops should be moved because they consume large amounts of nutrients, especially nitrogen.

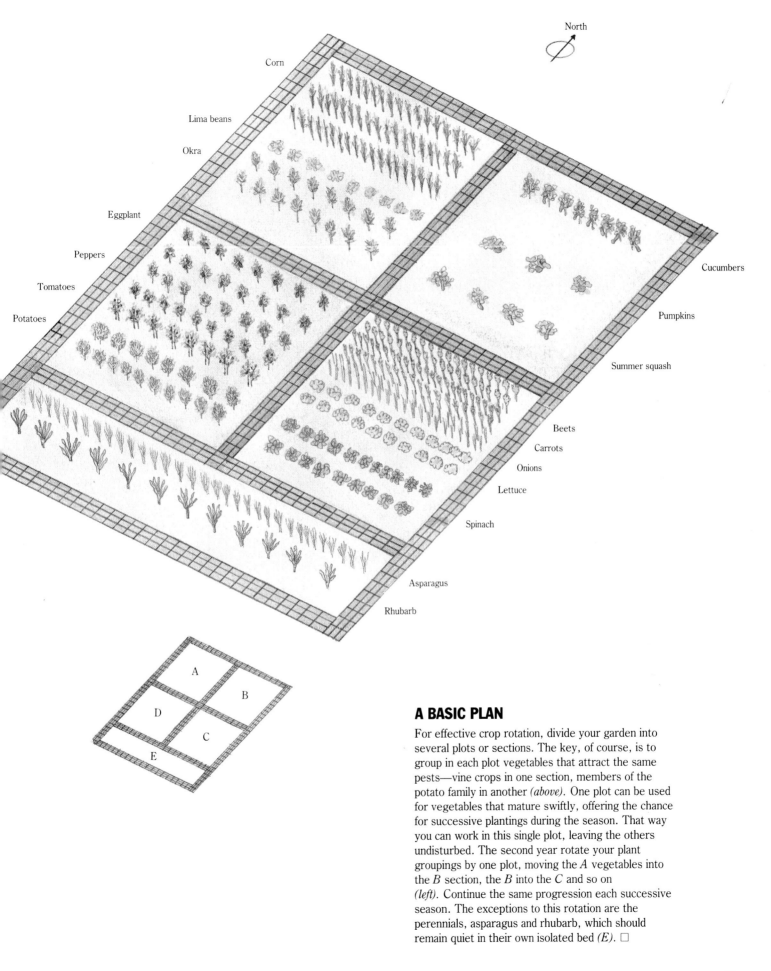

Corn

Lima beans

Okra

Eggplant

Peppers

Tomatoes

Potatoes

North

Cucumbers

Pumpkins

Summer squash

Beets

Carrots

Onions

Lettuce

Spinach

Asparagus

Rhubarb

A

B

D

C

E

A BASIC PLAN

For effective crop rotation, divide your garden into several plots or sections. The key, of course, is to group in each plot vegetables that attract the same pests—vine crops in one section, members of the potato family in another *(above)*. One plot can be used for vegetables that mature swiftly, offering the chance for successive plantings during the season. That way you can work in this single plot, leaving the others undisturbed. The second year rotate your plant groupings by one plot, moving the *A* vegetables into the *B* section, the *B* into the *C* and so on *(left)*. Continue the same progression each successive season. The exceptions to this rotation are the perennials, asparagus and rhubarb, which should remain quiet in their own isolated bed *(E)*. □

RELIEVING STRESS ON YOUNG TRANSPLANTS

For vegetable seedlings begun indoors, the move into the strong sun, brisk breezes and a garden full of busy pests can be hazardous and stressful. But there are several ways to ease the passage and get the seedlings off to a good start. One is a process called hardening off—gradually acclimating young plants to their new, rougher environment. About 10 days before the recommended time for transplanting arrives, move the seedlings outdoors for an hour, then for two hours the second day, then for three and so on until they have been in the sun for a full 10 hours. If you buy seedlings from a greenhouse, acclimate them the same way. If you buy them at a nursery, ask whether they have been hardened off. If they have not, harden them off before you plant them. This sort of gradual, gentle treatment is especially important for tender plants such as tomatoes, eggplant and peppers.

When they are ready for transplanting, choose a cool, cloudy day or a time in the late afternoon, when the sun is waning. Seedlings begun in peat pots can be planted pot and all; those begun in plastic cell packs should be watered and then removed before being set in the ground *(below and opposite)*. A good soaking diminishes stress and the root balls slip out of the containers more easily.

A strong, leafy young tomato plant wears a collar of newspaper to fend off cutworms. The paper will eventually crumble away, will not harm the plant and will prevent cutworms from climbing the stem.

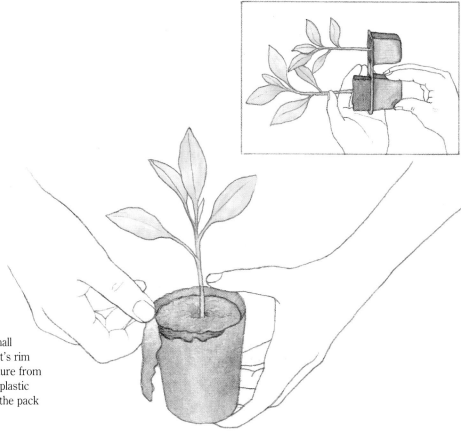

1 Before planting a seedling grown in a small peat pot, tear off about ½ inch of the pot's rim *(right);* an exposed rim will siphon moisture from the roots. To remove a seedling from a plastic cell pack *(inset),* squeeze the bottom of the pack gently and ease the plant out.

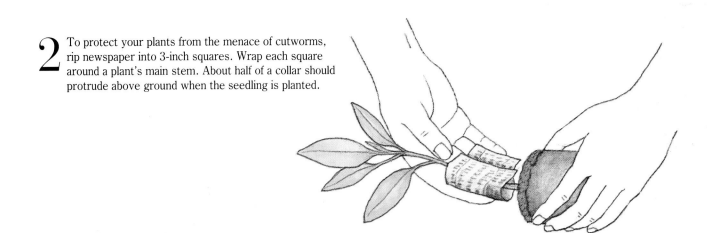

2 To protect your plants from the menace of cutworms, rip newspaper into 3-inch squares. Wrap each square around a plant's main stem. About half of a collar should protrude above ground when the seedling is planted.

3 To plant a seedling, dig a hole with a trowel a couple of inches deeper than the depth of the peat pot—or the root ball, if the seedling has been removed from its container. Into the bottom of the hole sprinkle ½ teaspoon of fertilizer. Cover the fertilizer with 2 inches of soil that has been well mixed with compost or a small amount of general-purpose fertilizer. Plant the seedling and firm the soil around it. Water immediately and then water some more for at least five days. □

TOMATOES ON THE SIDE

Tomato seedlings often become too tall and spindly. The best way to plant one of these precocious, leggy plants is on its side, the long stem in the ground and only 6 inches of foliage in the air. First, dig a small trench about 4 inches deep and as long as the stem. Sprinkle in some fertilizer and cover the fertilizer with a 2-inch layer of enriched soil. Remove any leaves from the stem and then lay it horizontally in the trench. Cover the roots and stem with more soil. The top 6 inches of foliage will soon turn upward toward the sun.

PREPARING THE GARDEN FOR SOWING

Evenly spaced and standing in an orderly row, bush bean seedlings sprout about two weeks after having been sown directly in garden soil.

Before you put seeds in the ground, make sure the soil has been properly tilled and amended. The texture should be fine and crumbly, moist but not soggy. Remove clods and stones; rake until the surface is smooth and level.

Test the temperature of the soil with a soil thermometer before sowing. Soil that is too cold will inhibit germination and stunt growth. If the soil temperature is below 65° F, lay a light mulch of leaves or straw over the soil and test again a few days later.

Lay out and mark seedbeds in straight rows, using stakes and string or a ready-made row marker, a device consisting of stakes with coiled string attached; you unwind the string as you walk along the row. For guidance on how deep to plant seeds, follow instructions on the seed packets. Seeds planted even a few inches deeper than recommended will not germinate.

After covering the seeds with soil, water the bed immediately, but use a light spray to avoid dislodging the seeds or disturbing the soil surface. Continue spraying to keep the ground moist during and after germination. To retain moisture and block intense sunlight, cover the seedbed with a thin layer of grass clippings or compost.

When seeds start to sprout, thin the seedlings to the spacing indicated on the seed packet; when overcrowded, they will never mature into healthy plants. Remove the least vigorous seedlings. Instead of pulling them up by the roots—which can damage nearby plants—cut them off at the base of the stem with a knife or a pair of scissors.

There are two ways to sow seeds outdoors. One is by hand; the other is with an all-in-one-operation wheel seeder like the one shown on page 35.

TESTING SOIL TEMPERATURE

To germinate, most summer vegetable seeds need to be planted in warm soil. A soil temperature of 75° F is just right for the majority. As soil temperatures dip toward 65° F, fewer seeds germinate, and the early growth and mature development of many crops is inhibited.

On a given day, air temperature and soil temperature may vary by 10 degrees or more. To get a reliable reading of the soil temperature, insert a soil thermometer into the ground to a depth of 2 to 3 inches. Delay planting if the soil is too cold. A light mulch of leaves or straw will keep the soil from drying out in the wind and from becoming waterlogged from spring rains.

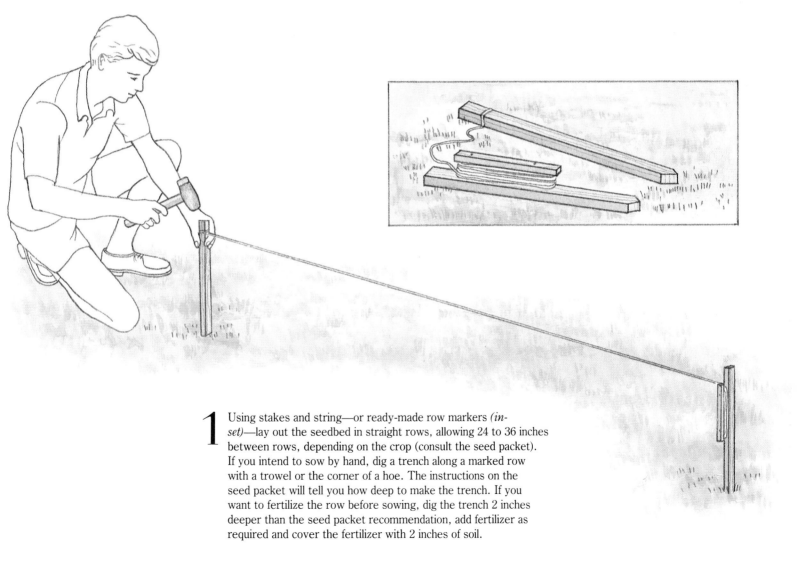

1 Using stakes and string—or ready-made row markers *(inset)*—lay out the seedbed in straight rows, allowing 24 to 36 inches between rows, depending on the crop (consult the seed packet). If you intend to sow by hand, dig a trench along a marked row with a trowel or the corner of a hoe. The instructions on the seed packet will tell you how deep to make the trench. If you want to fertilize the row before sowing, dig the trench 2 inches deeper than the seed packet recommendation, add fertilizer as required and cover the fertilizer with 2 inches of soil.

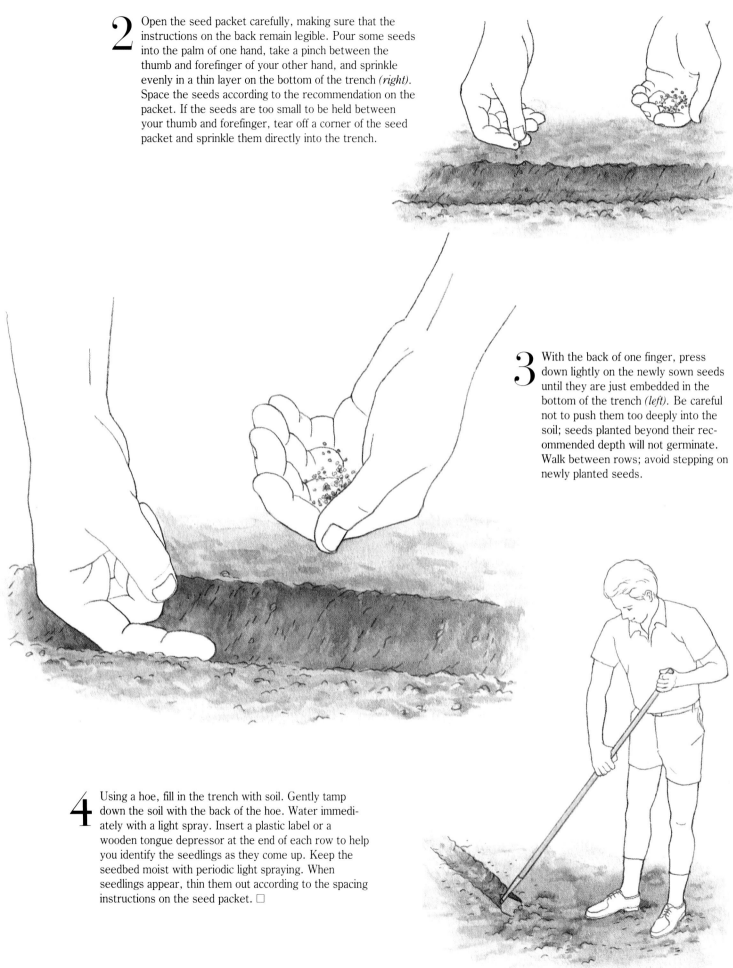

2 Open the seed packet carefully, making sure that the instructions on the back remain legible. Pour some seeds into the palm of one hand, take a pinch between the thumb and forefinger of your other hand, and sprinkle evenly in a thin layer on the bottom of the trench *(right)*. Space the seeds according to the recommendation on the packet. If the seeds are too small to be held between your thumb and forefinger, tear off a corner of the seed packet and sprinkle them directly into the trench.

3 With the back of one finger, press down lightly on the newly sown seeds until they are just embedded in the bottom of the trench *(left)*. Be careful not to push them too deeply into the soil; seeds planted beyond their recommended depth will not germinate. Walk between rows; avoid stepping on newly planted seeds.

4 Using a hoe, fill in the trench with soil. Gently tamp down the soil with the back of the hoe. Water immediately with a light spray. Insert a plastic label or a wooden tongue depressor at the end of each row to help you identify the seedlings as they come up. Keep the seedbed moist with periodic light spraying. When seedlings appear, thin them out according to the spacing instructions on the seed packet. □

ONE-STEP SOWING

A wheel seeder is a simple but ingenious device that allows you to combine all the steps involved in sowing seeds into a single operation. As you push the wheel seeder up and down each marked row *(right)*, it digs a trench to a preset depth, automatically drops and spaces the seeds, fills in the trench and tamps down the soil. You can buy many different models of wheel seeders at garden supply centers. But most share the features illustrated below.

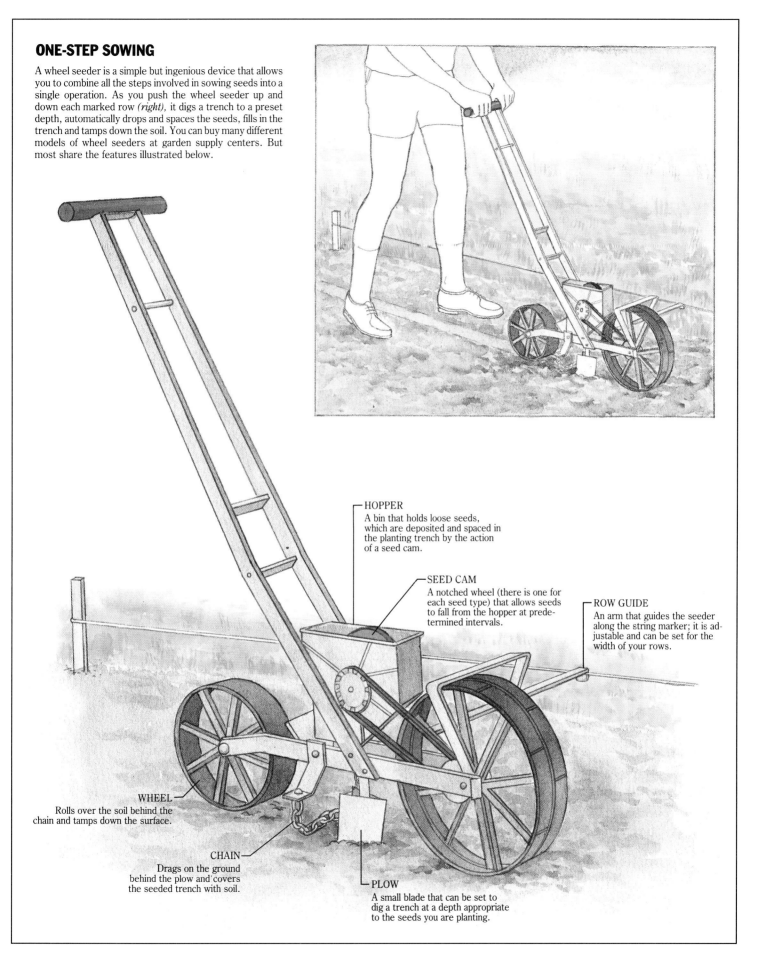

HOPPER
A bin that holds loose seeds, which are deposited and spaced in the planting trench by the action of a seed cam.

SEED CAM
A notched wheel (there is one for each seed type) that allows seeds to fall from the hopper at predetermined intervals.

ROW GUIDE
An arm that guides the seeder along the string marker; it is adjustable and can be set for the width of your rows.

WHEEL
Rolls over the soil behind the chain and tamps down the surface.

CHAIN
Drags on the ground behind the plow and covers the seeded trench with soil.

PLOW
A small blade that can be set to dig a trench at a depth appropriate to the seeds you are planting.

A TEPEE FRAME
FOR VINING PLANTS

Some vegetables do perfectly well on their own. But they do even better when they are given a helping hand from the gardener. A single cucumber vine, sprawling on the ground, may produce as many as 12 to 15 cucumbers a season, and the summer-long yield of a lone pole bean plant can easily come to about 2 gallons of beans.

When these meandering plants have an upright support, like the tepee-framed trellis shown here, their already abundant yield can actually be doubled. In addition, the plants take up less space and are less prone to attack by fungus and soilborne insects and diseases. As for the fruit, it is not only more abundant, but cleaner, better shaped and easier to harvest. The tepee even provides an added bonus: when lettuce and other tender greens are planted within its protective shade, they will thrive well past their normal growing season.

Besides cucumbers and pole beans, other vegetables that can be successfully grown vertically include lima beans and winter squash. Check the soil requirements of each plant type in the Dictionary of Vegetables *(pages 92-135),* and amend the soil accordingly before erecting the tepee. Also, check the seed packet for the depth at which the seeds must be set. For the tepee itself, you will need three 6- to 7-foot poles, tree branches or pieces of 2-by-2 lumber, plus a ball of nylon cord and a hammer or a mallet for driving the poles into the ground.

Pole beans grow on a tepee trellis. Since they climb rather than sprawl, the beans receive equal sun and ripen evenly. The trellis also saves space.

1 To construct the tepee, lash two poles together with nylon cord, using a figure-eight conformation. Position the cord about 5 or 6 inches in from one end of the poles. Then lash the third pole to the other two *(inset),* weaving the cord in and out among the three poles until they are securely joined. Knot the cord.

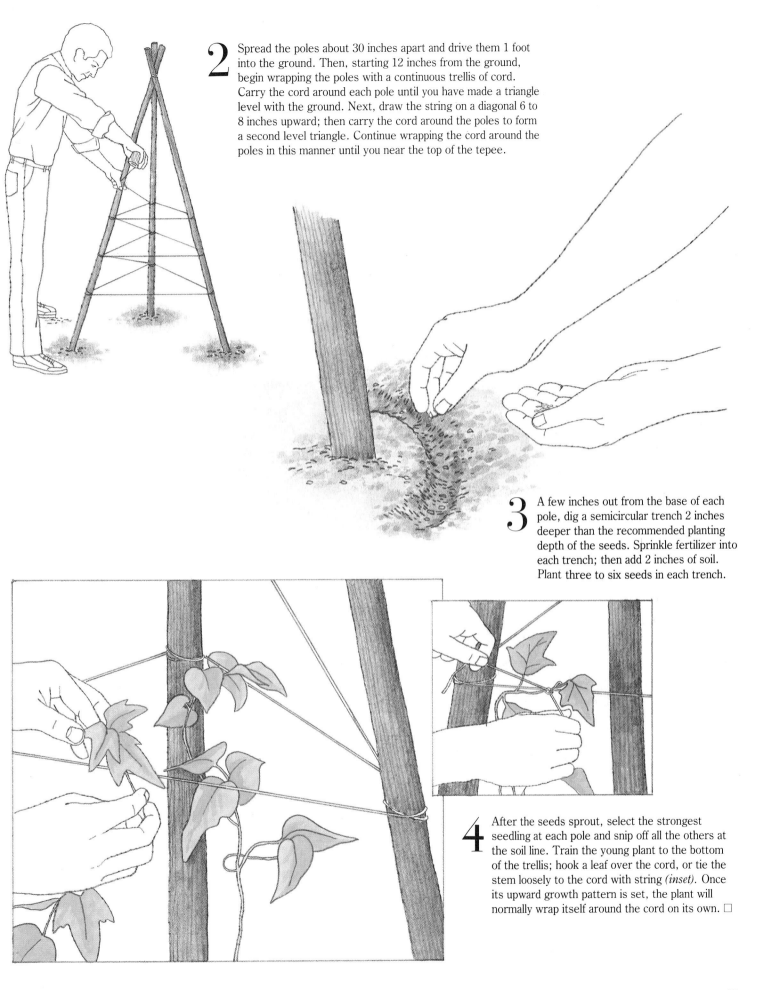

2 Spread the poles about 30 inches apart and drive them 1 foot into the ground. Then, starting 12 inches from the ground, begin wrapping the poles with a continuous trellis of cord. Carry the cord around each pole until you have made a triangle level with the ground. Next, draw the string on a diagonal 6 to 8 inches upward; then carry the cord around the poles to form a second level triangle. Continue wrapping the cord around the poles in this manner until you near the top of the tepee.

3 A few inches out from the base of each pole, dig a semicircular trench 2 inches deeper than the recommended planting depth of the seeds. Sprinkle fertilizer into each trench; then add 2 inches of soil. Plant three to six seeds in each trench.

4 After the seeds sprout, select the strongest seedling at each pole and snip off all the others at the soil line. Train the young plant to the bottom of the trellis; hook a leaf over the cord, or tie the stem loosely to the cord with string *(inset)*. Once its upward growth pattern is set, the plant will normally wrap itself around the cord on its own. □

INTERPLANTING CROPS FOR BONUS YIELDS

Wild grasses and other plants in an uncultivated field manage to prosper even though they often grow almost on top of one another. They survive the crowding in part because some of the plants shoot up early, mature swiftly and then die back, allowing their slower-growing neighbors an unimpeded chance at the sun.

This principle can be applied in a vegetable garden. A number of vegetables are spring growers and mature early. Others are best planted in midseason. You can overlap them, planting some midseason vegetables well before the early growers have finished producing. By the time the new plants need a full measure of space, light and air, the older ones will have gone to seed.

This technique, called interplanting, makes maximum use of a garden's space and can dramatically increase its yield. And it can be done with a variety of crops. Green peppers grow with lettuce in the photograph at right; the drawings show how to interplant peppers with broccoli. For other successful pairings, see the box on the opposite page.

A parallel method of extending a garden's harvest is to stagger the times certain crops mature. Planting a few summer squash on, say, June 15 and then another batch on July 1 will produce two separate crops a couple of weeks apart. Similarly, the harvest can be lengthened by planting several different versions of the same vegetable at the same time. Some hybrid corns, for example, ripen in only 54 days; others take as long as 80 days. Growing both ensures a long season of sweet, homegrown corn.

The shiny green leaves of young sweet pepper plants emerge between rows of butterhead lettuce (bottom) and red leaf lettuce (top). Both lettuces will have been harvested long before the peppers mature.

1 To interplant green pepper seedlings with mature broccoli plants, first use a trowel to clear away any weeds that have grown up, then make room for the peppers by trimming the lower broccoli leaves with a knife or garden shears as shown.

2 Dig holes for the seedlings in a staggered pattern between broccoli plants *(inset, below).* To the soil you have removed, add organic matter. Sprinkle fertilizer in the holes, then pour in some amended soil. Put a seedling in each hole, add more soil and tamp lightly. Water well.

3 After a few weeks, if your timing has been right, the pepper seedlings should have begun to mature— and the broccoli plants will have ceased yielding. At that stage, remove the older plants by cutting them off at ground level. Do not bother to dig up the roots; let them stay in the ground to rot, and thus enrich the garden soil. □

GOOD COMBINATIONS

Cucumbers and Peppers
Spinach and Onions
Broccoli and Peppers
Carrots and Beets or Radishes
Corn and Squash or Cucumbers
Lettuce and Onions, Radishes or Beets
Tomatoes and Chives or Parsley

ASPARAGUS:
A PERENNIAL SPRING TREAT

Crisp asparagus spears shoot up shortly after the ground has thawed. Spears are ready for harvest when they are 6 to 8 inches high. They should be cut off at ground level with a knife—but carefully, so that the blade does not slice into roots or spears forming underground.

Grown since ancient times—the emperor Nero was an early connoisseur—asparagus is treasured not only because it is the first green vegetable to pop up each spring and a delectable one, but also because its tender spears grow of their own accord year after year. Unlike most other vegetables, asparagus is a perennial and a hardy one at that. Well cared for beds produce for 15 years and more.

Such a marvel naturally has its quirks. Asparagus thrives only where winters have enough bite to cause freezing, since the roots must become dormant to renew themselves. That rules out the Deep South (Florida and Louisiana, for example) and other warm regions. Yet asparagus plants need plenty of hot summer sun. A bed should be located in full sunlight, and in a spot where there is shelter from chill spring winds.

Asparagus also requires a good deal of space. Growing enough to satisfy the appetites of a family of four takes two rows about 20 feet long and spaced at least 4 feet apart. The soil should be light, loose and well drained. Planting should be done in the spring. In buying stock to plant, select the largest one-year-old crowns your nursery has for sale. They should look crisp and have moist, healthy roots. How to cultivate a bed and plant the rows is shown at right and on the following pages.

A last quirk of asparagus is that the roots must mature in the ground for two years before spears are harvested. None should be cut the year of planting and few, if any, the next spring. The third year spears can be cut for four weeks. After that, asparagus can be harvested for six to eight weeks each spring.

The uncut spears of the first years, and some every year afterward, should be allowed to continue growing. They will form handsome ferny bushes about 5 feet tall. Besides being decorative, the foliage creates sugars that, stored in the roots through the winter, increase the next spring's crop. When the bushes turn brown in the fall, they should be cut back—and added to the compost pile to make mulch for another season.

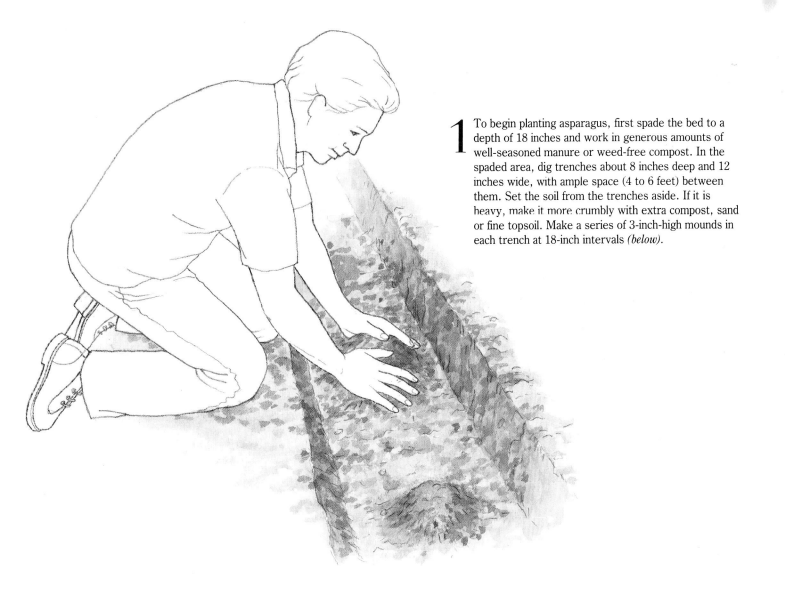

1 To begin planting asparagus, first spade the bed to a depth of 18 inches and work in generous amounts of well-seasoned manure or weed-free compost. In the spaded area, dig trenches about 8 inches deep and 12 inches wide, with ample space (4 to 6 feet) between them. Set the soil from the trenches aside. If it is heavy, make it more crumbly with extra compost, sand or fine topsoil. Make a series of 3-inch-high mounds in each trench at 18-inch intervals *(below)*.

2 Gently hold the crown you have bought and snip off any broken or rotted roots with a garden clipper. Then trim the roots again, removing a maximum of 2 or 3 inches, to make them roughly equal in length. Note: nurseries often sell crowns that are two and three years old. Avoid them. Although large, they do not produce a crop any sooner than one-year-old crowns, can carry disease and are harder to plant successfully.

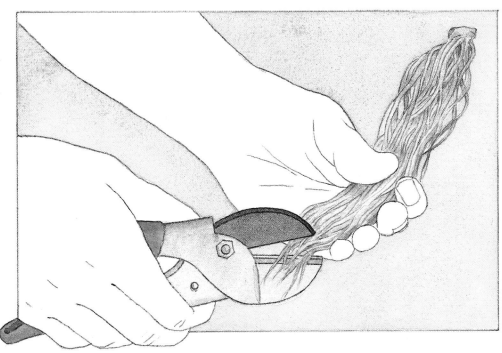

3 Place the crowns over the soil mounds you have made in the trenches. Spread the roots apart carefully. It is important that the soil in the trenches be free of weeds; asparagus suffers from the competition weeds offer for water and nutrients. Large ones entangled in asparagus roots are particularly harmful.

4 Cover each crown with 3 inches of the soil that was dug from the trench. Gently sprinkle the mounds with water. Moderate but frequent watering works best. You do not want to flood the trenches, and asparagus roots do not thrive if they are too wet.

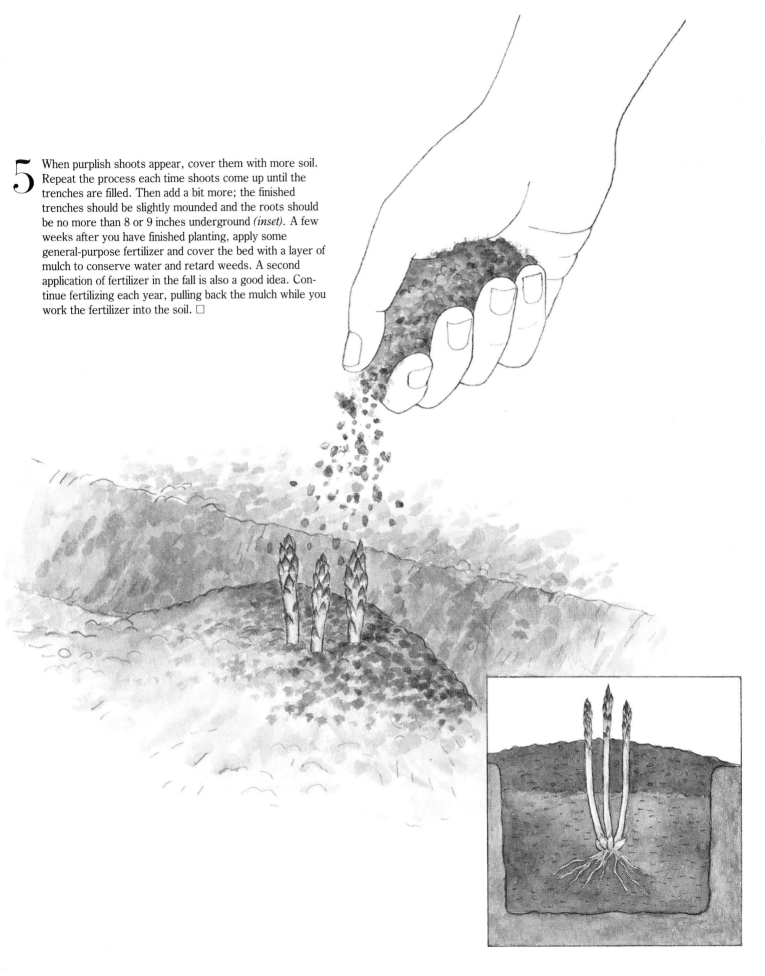

5 When purplish shoots appear, cover them with more soil. Repeat the process each time shoots come up until the trenches are filled. Then add a bit more; the finished trenches should be slightly mounded and the roots should be no more than 8 or 9 inches underground *(inset)*. A few weeks after you have finished planting, apply some general-purpose fertilizer and cover the bed with a layer of mulch to conserve water and retard weeds. A second application of fertilizer in the fall is also a good idea. Continue fertilizing each year, pulling back the mulch while you work the fertilizer into the soil. □

A RAISED VEGETABLE BED:
ALL-PURPOSE PROBLEM SOLVER

Cornstalks, carrot tops, lettuces and other vegetable greens stand together in a raised bed—along with a row of marigolds, which help repel bugs.

A primary requirement of a lush vegetable harvest is good, rich soil that has adequate drainage. But all too often backyards turn out to have crusty, clayey earth that produces little in exchange for a lot of hard digging. And inadequate drainage can mean waterlogged roots, which in turn mean rotted plants.

Both of these problems are easily solved by a raised garden bed—a planting area built up above normal ground level. Such an elevated garden plot can be filled with easy-to-work soil. Because it is elevated, a raised bed will drain well. It will be deep enough for all sorts of vegetables and particularly useful for root crops *(pages 46-47)*.

To construct a raised bed, outline the area with stakes and string. The bed can be any length, but no more than 6 feet wide, so that all parts of it will be within easy reach. Buy lengths of 6-by-6 landscape timbers of rot-resistant redwood or cedar. Also obtain some wire mesh (to keep out tunneling animals). Lay the timbers in two courses alongside the stakes and string, and bolt them together. Prepare the soil for planting as shown in the drawings opposite.

1 Step inside the raised bed and, with a spade or a garden fork, turn over the earth to a depth of about 6 inches. This will help the bottom layers of soil within the bed to drain. After digging, do not bother to smooth the area; leaving the earth churned up will help water to drain through.

2 Cut wire mesh to cover an area slightly larger than that enclosed by the timber framework; allow 4 to 6 inches extra in length and width. Bend the extra wire upward to close off the space between timbers and soil, and attach it to the wood with a staple gun.

3 Fill the frame with a growing mixture. The best and easiest method is to shovel in a layer of good soil, then a layer of aged manure, then more soil—and so on until the bed is filled to within 2 inches of the top. Sprinkle an all-purpose fertilizer evenly over the bed and work it into the soil. Rake the bed smooth and level, water it—and plant your seeds. □

PREPARING A BED
FOR ROOT CROPS

Sporting leafy green tops—which make them easy to grasp at harvest time—carrots emerge from soft loam. Root crops can generally grow close together and are good vegetables for limited spaces.

Vegetables that are grown for their edible roots—carrots, beets, parsnips—are among the tastiest and most healthful of all vegetables. They also offer some practical advantages to the home gardener. They have the effect of lengthening the summer growing season. Most can be planted earlier in the spring than other vegetables because, lodged snugly underground, they do not suffer from the season's last, frosty cold snaps. Similarly, they continue growing, waiting to be harvested, even after the first hard frosts of autumn have shriveled most other crops. And after having been harvested, they keep remarkably well. They stay fresh for months if they are stored in a cold cellar or in some other cool place, so they provide homegrown vegetables for the table throughout the winter.

Because the roots are the most important part of these vegetables, good soil conditions are critical. A raised bed *(pages 44-45)* is ideal: it has good drainage and the roots will develop undisturbed by underground rocks and hard, compacted earth. But root crops can also be started from seed in any well-prepared area of the garden.

For an easy start, the seeds should be planted in a light, loose growing medium such as a mixture of vermiculite and dry peat moss *(opposite),* which allows the roots to grow evenly and without resistance.

In establishing their nourishing roots, these plants consume soil nutrients at a rapid clip, so before planting them it is a good idea to sprinkle fertilizer on the bed and work it into the soil with a spade. The type of fertilizer used depends on the particular vegetable being planted. After the planting is done, the bed should be mulched, to retard weeds and conserve moisture, and treated to frequent waterings.

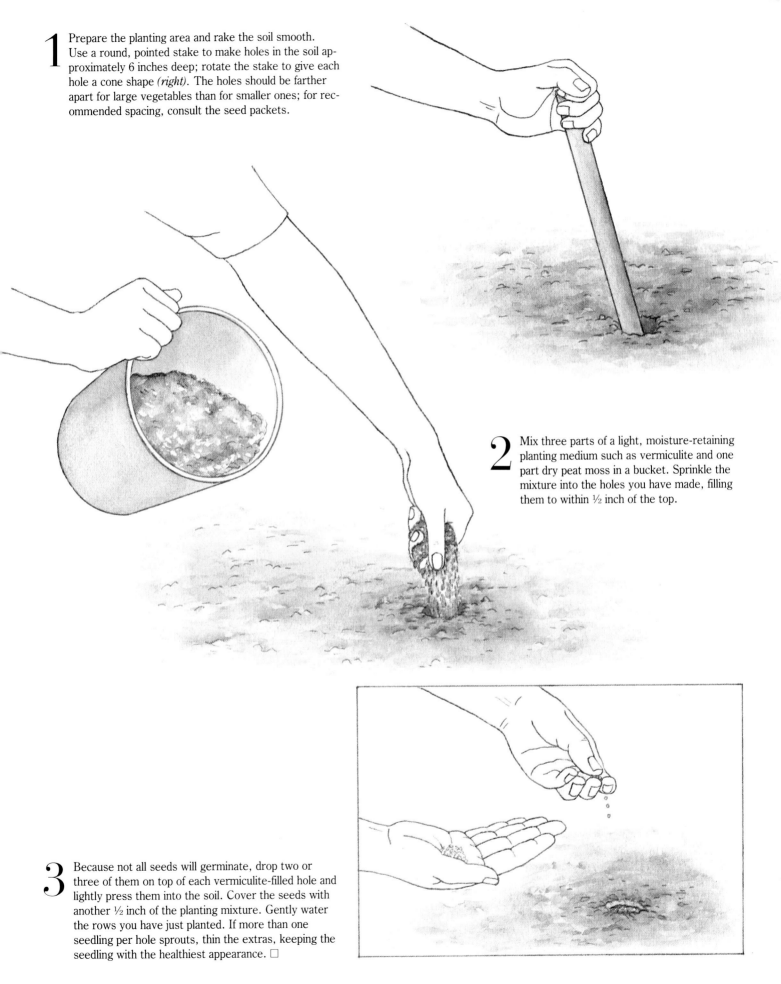

1 Prepare the planting area and rake the soil smooth. Use a round, pointed stake to make holes in the soil approximately 6 inches deep; rotate the stake to give each hole a cone shape *(right)*. The holes should be farther apart for large vegetables than for smaller ones; for recommended spacing, consult the seed packets.

2 Mix three parts of a light, moisture-retaining planting medium such as vermiculite and one part dry peat moss in a bucket. Sprinkle the mixture into the holes you have made, filling them to within ½ inch of the top.

3 Because not all seeds will germinate, drop two or three of them on top of each vermiculite-filled hole and lightly press them into the soil. Cover the seeds with another ½ inch of the planting mixture. Gently water the rows you have just planted. If more than one seedling per hole sprouts, thin the extras, keeping the seedling with the healthiest appearance. □

GROWING POTATOES UNDER STRAW

Americans consume a staggering 128 pounds of potatoes per person per year. And there are good reasons why this is so. The potato is tasty on its own, but its flavor is subtle and able to blend with the flavors of almost any other foods it is served with. It is also rich in vitamins and iron.

The home gardener can easily grow potatoes. They are best grown from so-called seed potatoes—potatoes that have been cut into pieces and planted so that their eyes, or buds, will sprout new leaves, stems, roots and tubers.

If you plant seed potatoes, it is better to buy specially prepared seed potatoes from a garden center or through mail order than to use grocery store potatoes. Special seed potatoes are certified healthy and free of disease; grocery store potatoes may be carrying disease without showing it, and they may have been treated to prevent sprouting.

Seed potatoes can be started in either of two ways. One is to plant them in hilled rows, the same way that corn is planted *(page 64)*. The other is to lay them on top of the soil—either on the ground or in a raised bed—with a covering of straw *(opposite)*. In the latter method, the potatoes will grow only about half as big as ones sown in the soil and hilled, but you will get more of them—especially if you live in an area where soil drainage is slow or one where the soil is rocky, such as New England. Just make sure you use straw (which is dried wheat, and seed-free), not hay (which is dried grass, and full of seeds).

A blanket of straw conceals a crop of new potatoes —their ripening signaled by the lush green leaves that have surfaced above the insulating straw.

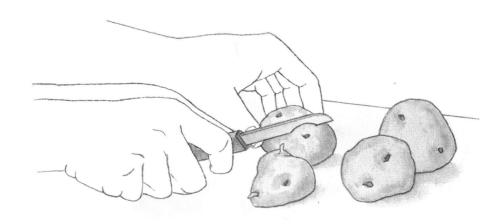

1 Cut seed potatoes into chunks about 1½ inches thick, making sure that each chunk has at least one eye. Small potatoes may be left whole, but slice a bit off one side to serve as a bottom so the seed potato will stay put when laid on the soil. Leave the pieces in a warm place for a day or two so the cut surfaces can heal and dry.

2 Prepare the soil by working in organic matter and fertilizer. Rake the bed smooth. Place the potato pieces on the soil, 12 to 15 inches apart, with the cut side down and the eyes pointing upward and outward *(right)*. Press each piece firmly into the soil about ½ inch deep.

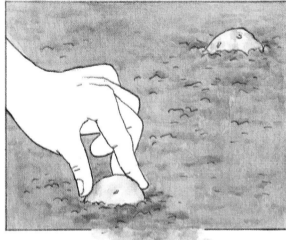

3 Cover the bed with about 18 inches of clean straw. If the bed is in a windy location, cover the straw with about ½ inch of soil to hold it in place. Water regularly to keep the soil from drying out; if it does the potatoes are likely to be knobby. □

A DEVELOPING POTATO PLANT

About 13 weeks after planting under straw, a seed potato has sent up some upright stems with leafy green foliage. Along the soil line it has formed specialized stems with swellings called tubers. These are a fresh crop of potatoes. From both the stems and the tubers, many hairlike feeder roots descend into the soil to absorb nutrients.

3
TENDING
YOUR GARDEN

There's more to maintaining a garden than routine chores and simple patience. You will get the most out of your vegetable garden if you pay close attention to the requirements of different crops—and if you are prepared to take action to satisfy those needs. Lending vegetables a helping hand at the right time can actually reduce the amount of work you have to do in your garden in the long run. It's much easier to smother weeds before they appear than it is to pull them up later; it's more efficient to strengthen a tender young shoot than to prop up a top-heavy stalk; it's easier, more efficient and a lot more satisfying to arrange for the right amounts of sun and water and the right kind of protection against insects and disease than it is to try to salvage sun-scalded, desiccated or pest-ridden seedlings.

On the following pages, you will find step-by-step instructions that show you how to shade leafy greens like lettuce, how to support and train tall-growing crops like tomatoes, and how to provide water and mulch for the most popular garden vegetables. There is an age-old technique for raising corn that was practiced by the American Indians; another, for controlling weeds and keeping soil warm by means of black plastic, is as recent an innovation as the synthetics industry. All of these techniques are easy to learn and easy to put into practice, and all are designed with the same goal in mind: to ensure that the vegetables you plant in the spring will ripen into flavorful, healthful complements to your table when harvest time comes in the fall.

SHADING LETTUCE FROM MIDSUMMER SUN

Lettuce and other leafy vegetables like the sun—in moderation. They do best in the spring and the fall when the days are a mix of sun and shade. In the intense heat of the midsummer sun, these cool-season crops may bolt—produce flowers—after which the leaves turn bitter and wilt. The combination of heat, humidity and intense sunlight causes leaf pores to open, which makes the leaves susceptible to pollutants in the air. High heat and fluctuating levels of soil moisture can cause tip burn, a condition in which leaf edges turn brown and may eventually die.

You can take steps to protect the leaves, however. To keep your lettuce growing and harvestable throughout the summer, shelter the plants beneath a temporary shade structure that will shield them from direct sunlight and from high temperatures.

A typical shade structure consists of white screening material—cheesecloth is ideal —stretched across a semirigid framework. The screening material must be thin enough to let light through while blocking much of the sun's heat. The framework must be sturdy enough to withstand winds.

Butterhead lettuce flourishes in a partially shaded garden patch. Lettuce and other leafy vegetables need some protection from hot summer sun and can grow successfully in the shade of taller plants.

1 To build a temporary shade structure that will keep lettuce cool in hot weather, drive four stakes into the ground to a depth of 1 foot with a mallet or a hammer. The stakes should be 4½ to 5 feet long. Use 2-by-2 lumber or branches stripped of foliage. To strengthen the framework, nail another 2-by-2 or branch to the tops of two stakes along one of the short sides of the structure *(right)*. Then nail a matching crossbeam to the pair of stakes on the opposite side of the lettuce patch.

2 Connect the crossbeams with two or three lengths of tightly tied nylon string *(left)*. Space the string so that it will support sun-screening material over the entire lettuce patch.

3 Drape cheesecloth or an old sheet over the structure so that it overlaps the crossbeams and the string on all sides. To keep it from blowing away in the wind, lay two sticks across the width of the sun-screening material parallel to the crossbeams. □

DRIP IRRIGATION—
WATER WHERE IT COUNTS

Almost no other care you give your vegetables is more important than watering. Not only do fresh vegetables consist mostly of water, but nutrients from the soil must be dissolved in water before they can enter the growing plant.

Plants take in water through their roots, so make sure the soil is moistened to a depth of 4 to 5 inches. To tell if your plants are getting enough water, dig down to the base of the roots with a trowel and scoop up some soil. If it feels moist, you have watered sufficiently. Do not overwater; saturated soil keeps air from reaching the roots, and without air the roots will rot and die. Also, wet soil attracts slugs and snails.

If you water with an ordinary garden hose, do your watering in the morning, if possible, to allow the foliage to dry out by nightfall; at night, wet leaves tend to mildew.

A far better way to water is by drip irrigation, a method that lets water seep at a measured rate to many plant roots simultaneously. Drip irrigation doesn't wet plant leaves, and water is not lost to evaporation. The apparatus you need, available at garden centers and by mail order, usually consists of an irrigation hose—one with several openings from which small, flexible minihoses, or ooze tubes, branch off to deliver water directly to the roots of individual plants. Most such systems can be connected to an ordinary garden hose *(below and opposite)*. And most come with instructions telling you how long to let them run to water a given area, and with the parts needed to put the hose together.

To determine how much irrigation hose you will need, draw a plan of your garden; measure the length of each row and of all turns between rows.

Lying on either side of a row of tomato plants, a drip irrigation hose with ooze tubes lets water seep slowly into the soil where plants need it most— at their roots. Such a system is efficient because hardly any water is lost to evaporation.

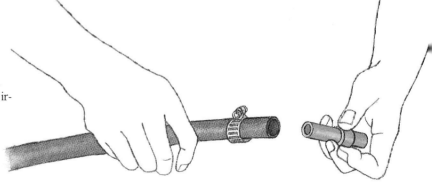

1 To assemble a drip irrigation system, first slip a clamp loosely around one end of the irrigation hose; then insert a plug *(right)*. Tighten the clamp around the plug with a screwdriver to seal the end of the hose.

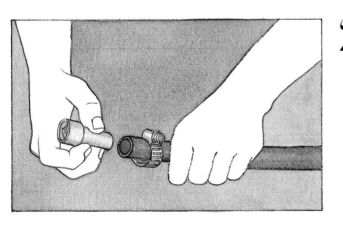

2 Slip a clamp loosely around the other end of the irrigation hose. Insert a female hose coupling *(left)*; tighten the clamp over the coupling. Connect this coupling to your garden hose.

3 Run the irrigation hose along the furrows lying between rows of vegetables, making a smooth curve at each end *(right)*. Smooth out any kinks in the hose and avoid right angles. Continue laying the irrigation hose until it lies alongside all plants to be watered.

4 Following the manufacturer's instructions, punch holes (using an awl or the tip of a nail if necessary) at intervals that coincide with the plants that need watering. Insert thin ooze tubes into the holes in the irrigation hose *(left)*.

5 Place the water-emitting end of an ooze tube on the ground directly under each plant *(below)* so that water soaks down to the plant's roots. Turn on the tap daily as recommended by the manufacturer's instructions. □

WATERING A LONE PLANT

To keep a single plant well watered, punch holes in the sides and the bottom of a plastic milk jug and sink it into the ground near the plant. The top of the jug should protrude about 1 inch above the ground. Fill it from a watering can or a hose. Water will seep into the soil to the roots. Refill the jug when the soil feels dry.

PLASTIC MULCH
FOR WEED CONTROL

Sweet potato plants spread their leaves above a protective sheet of black plastic. By conserving water, holding heat and eliminating weeds, plastic mulch gives vegetables a head start on the growing season.

What's good for one plant in a garden tends to be good for other plants. That's why it can be difficult to encourage the growth of vegetables while discouraging the growth of weeds. Fortunately, there is one way to do both at the same time: lay down a mulch.

A mulch is any layer of material, organic or inorganic, that you place on the ground around plants. Mulches not only keep weed seeds from germinating by blocking sunlight, they conserve moisture by inhibiting evaporation and act as insulation against extremes in soil temperature.

Organic mulches, such as well-rotted compost, hay, shredded leaves, ground corncobs and bark chips, also improve soil texture and fertility. But they have drawbacks as well; hay harbors weed seeds, bark can be infested with ants and termites, and some organic mulches actually leach nitrogen from the soil as they decompose.

Inorganic mulches range from old newspapers to large rolls of aluminum foil and black plastic available at garden centers. A major drawback of paper and foil is that they look unnatural in a garden; foil is also costly and hard to handle.

Many home gardeners mulch with plastic because it is inexpensive, easy to install and unsurpassed for weed control. Laid down at planting time, sheets of plastic also keep foliage clean, which can prevent disease; by helping to warm the soil, a plastic mulch can hasten the ripening of warm-season crops like peppers and tomatoes by as much as 14 days.

Black plastic sheets are relatively unobtrusive; to hide them entirely, cover them with a thin layer of organic material. Plastic mulch is sold in rolls 1½ to 3 feet wide, just right for a broad row of vegetables.

1 After tilling and preparing the soil for planting, use a rake to build a low mound of soil the length of the row *(left)*. Rake the soil up from the two long sides, leaving a shallow depression on either side. Smooth the soil on top of the mound. Remove clods and large stones.

2 Unroll a length of black plastic mulch to match the length of the row *(right)*. Secure the plastic at one end with a few small stones and drape it over the earthen mound. Use a pair of scissors to cut the roll to fit.

3 With your fingers, work the edge of the plastic sheet into the ground on both sides of the row and at the ends to a depth of 2 inches *(right)*. To anchor the plastic against wind and rain, push loose soil over the edge of the sheet and tamp it down.

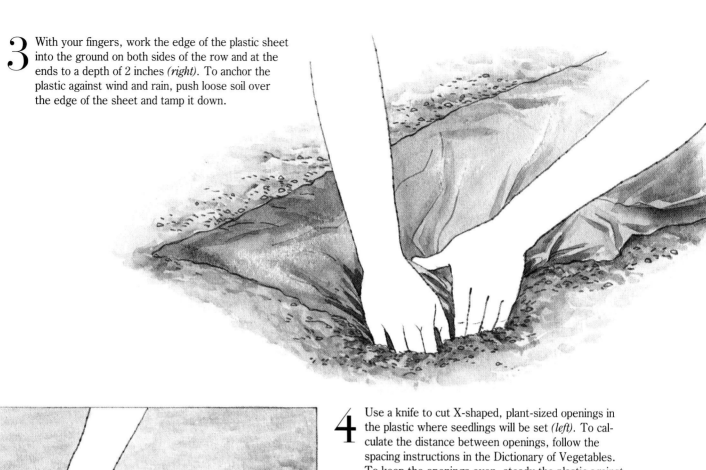

4 Use a knife to cut X-shaped, plant-sized openings in the plastic where seedlings will be set *(left)*. To calculate the distance between openings, follow the spacing instructions in the Dictionary of Vegetables. To keep the openings even, steady the plastic against the ground with one hand while cutting.

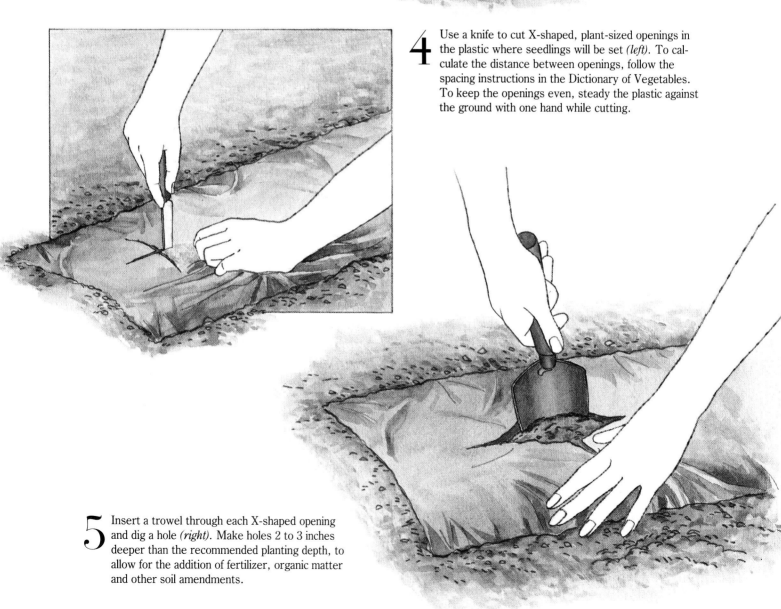

5 Insert a trowel through each X-shaped opening and dig a hole *(right)*. Make holes 2 to 3 inches deeper than the recommended planting depth, to allow for the addition of fertilizer, organic matter and other soil amendments.

6 Fill each hole with water to give the soil a good soaking. Let the water drain out the bottom of each hole. Since the plastic mulch will inhibit evaporation from the soil surface, much of the water will remain available to the roots of the plant as it grows. Continue digging holes and filling them with water until you have completed the row.

7 When the water in the first hole has drained away, add about 2 tablespoons of complete fertilizer. This is fertilizer that contains the three major plant nutrients—nitrogen, phosphorus and potassium—in percentages listed on the label (for example, 5-10-5). To guard the roots from direct contact with the fertilizer, cover them with at least 2 inches of soil mixed with organic matter. Insert the seedling. Fill in the hole with enriched soil and gently firm with your fingers. □

STAKES AND CAGES
TO SUPPORT TOMATOES

The tomato is the most popular home garden crop in America —partly because it tastes good, partly because it is one of the easiest crops to grow. It is also among the most diverse of crops; it comes in several hundred varieties. Yet all of those varieties can be divided into two general types: what horticulturalists call "determinate" and "indeterminate."

Determinate tomatoes are so called because they are bushlike in form and generally yield a single crop of fruit. Indeterminate tomatoes—the more common of the two—have vinelike growth habits; they sprawl in any direction where they meet no interference, and with sufficient sun, water and nutrients they will keep growing and producing fruit until the first frost of autumn.

Which kind of tomato you plant will influence how you grow them in your garden. Indeterminate tomatoes can be left to sprawl, but if they are they will be susceptible to rot, disease and insect pests. You can minimize these dangers if you stake the plants *(page 63)*. Staking has the further advantage of saving space; stakes can be set as close as 18 inches apart, whereas a sprawling plant may cover as much as 8 feet of ground. If you stake, however, you must prune the plants regularly every week to ensure vigorous growth. And as the plant rises in height, the new growth must be repeatedly tied to help keep the plant vertical.

Determinate tomatoes can be allowed without risk to stand on their own. They cannot, however, be staked; they are all too compact and many are too short.

For all indeterminate tomatoes, and for determinate tomatoes that grow from 2 to 3 feet tall, there is a third alternative —caging *(opposite)*. Caging requires a minimum of pruning. It also does away with the need for repeated tying; the cages serve to contain the plants as they grow.

You can buy tomato cages at a garden center or make your own from pieces of wire mesh *(inset, opposite)*.

Red 'Celebrity' tomatoes ripen inside a wire mesh cage, which supports the plant as it grows tall and keeps the tomatoes within easy reach for harvesting.

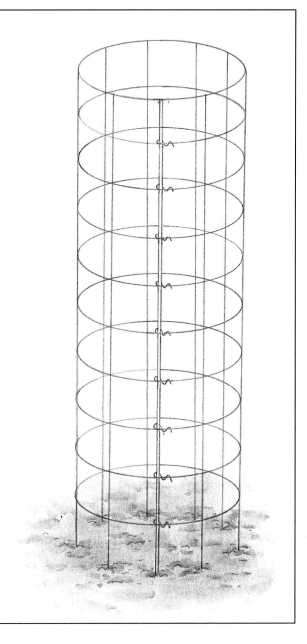

AN ENCIRCLING CAGE

To make your own cage for a tomato plant, buy a 5-foot square of concrete-reinforcing wire mesh. The holes should be 6-inch squares to allow you to pick and remove large tomatoes through the mesh. Bring two edges of the mesh together to make a cylinder and secure them by twisting the horizontal wires that protrude from one edge around the wires on the other edge *(inset, above)*. The diameter of the cylinder will be between 18 and 24 inches. With a wire cutter, cut off the last horizontal wire on the bottom end of the cylinder, leaving vertical wire "spikes" *(right)* that can be pushed into the ground to anchor the cage.

1 When a tomato seedling has had time to establish itself outdoors—about three weeks after transplanting—prepare it for caging. Use a clean, sharp knife to cut off the less vigorous shoots near the base of the plant; leave one or two strong main stems. By concentrating the plant's energy in fewer stems, you will increase the yield of tomatoes later on.

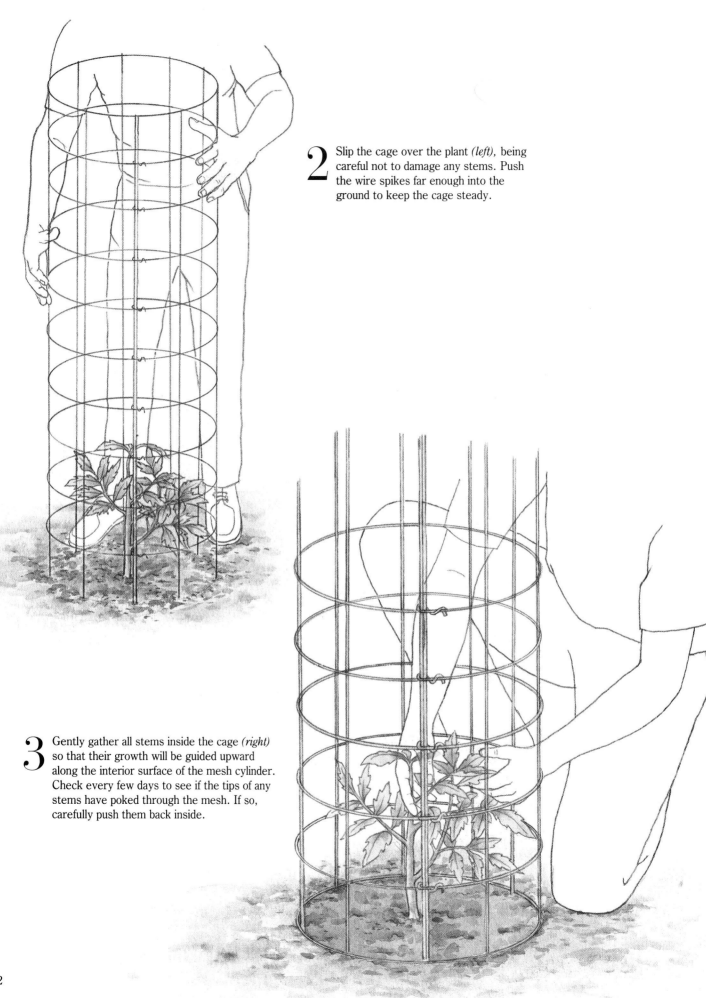

2 Slip the cage over the plant *(left)*, being careful not to damage any stems. Push the wire spikes far enough into the ground to keep the cage steady.

3 Gently gather all stems inside the cage *(right)* so that their growth will be guided upward along the interior surface of the mesh cylinder. Check every few days to see if the tips of any stems have poked through the mesh. If so, carefully push them back inside.

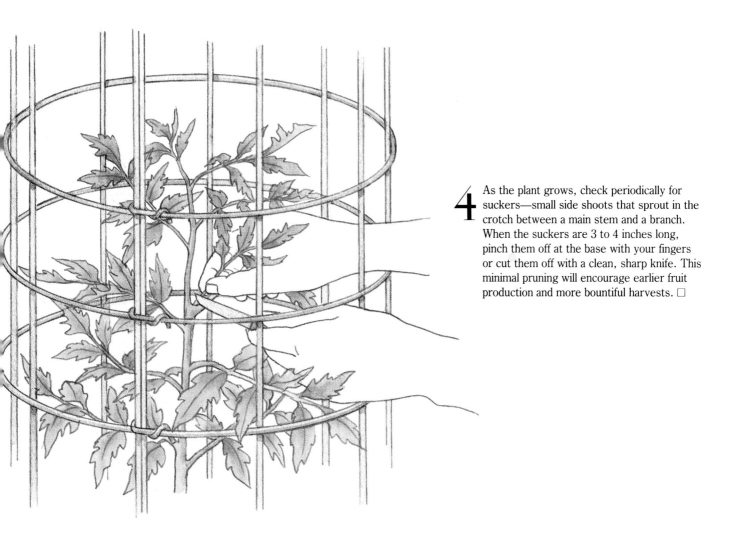

4 As the plant grows, check periodically for suckers—small side shoots that sprout in the crotch between a main stem and a branch. When the suckers are 3 to 4 inches long, pinch them off at the base with your fingers or cut them off with a clean, sharp knife. This minimal pruning will encourage earlier fruit production and more bountiful harvests. □

A TIMELY STAKE

To stake a tomato plant, insert a 6-foot wooden stake into the ground about 4 inches from the plant when it is a three-week-old seedling. Drive the stake 10 inches deep. Tie the plant to the stake with a length of soft cord or plastic-covered twist tie. First loop the cord tightly around the stake so that it will not slip down. Then loop it loosely around the stem, just below a branch or bud, leaving ½ inch of slack; this will keep the cord from choking the stem as it grows thicker. Check periodically; add a new tie whenever the plant grows another foot.

MOUNDING SOIL FOR STRONG CORNSTALKS

Five weeks after planting, corn growing in neat rows is about 18 inches tall. The sweetest varieties take up to 12 weeks to mature.

Corn has been a staple of the American diet ever since the Indians taught the Pilgrims to grow it, and it has been cultivated in much the same way since then. For example, settlers learned to "hill" corn—to make mounds around the bases of the stalks to support them—and this is still done today *(opposite)*. Farmers have long known that a first crop can be planted early—even before the last spring frost—because the young plants can stand some cold. But corn also needs lots of warmth and should get full, day-long sun. Corn also soaks up nutrients, and a nitrogen-rich fertilizer should be worked into the soil. Then the seeds should be planted in furrows 2 inches deep and 36 inches apart. Plant five seeds per foot; not all will germinate, and extra plants can be snipped off when they are about 6 inches high *(opposite, top)*.

Seeds of one particular variety should not be planted in a single long row, but rather in a compact block of several shorter rows. The plants pollinate each other to produce ears and they need to be close together. By the same token, different varieties should be kept far apart; cross-pollination between them can spoil the ears' taste and texture.

A last trick: a single planting of corn produces ears for only about one week, so if you want to have corn all summer, plant several crops two weeks apart until 12 weeks before the first frost in your area.

1 When your corn has grown 6 or 8 inches tall, thin your rows so that the remaining plants are about 8 inches apart. The stalks you cut should be snipped off at ground level; the roots can be left to rot in the ground.

2 After thinning the rows, rake between them *(above)*, breaking up any clods, smoothing the soil and getting rid of weeds. The raking should also loosen about 1 inch of soil, which makes hilling *(below)* easier.

3 To hill your corn, pull loose earth up and around the stalks with a regular hoe, forming 3-inch mounds. Work at the rows from both sides to be sure the stalks get support all around. Do not chop the earth too close to the stalks; you can injure the roots. The hilling process—both raking and hoeing—should be repeated when the stalks are about 1 foot tall. □

4
HARVESTING YOUR CROPS

hakespeare said, "Ripeness is all." But to a gardener, ripeness is a relative term. Some vegetables, like
sprouts, are grown especially to be harvested young, long
before the plants reach their natural maturity. Other
crops, like potatoes, can be harvested both when they
are young and and when they are mature—with markedly different results in taste and texture. The squash family offers an
entire range of varieties for early and late harvesting; each
variety must be handled differently.

Knowing when a particular vegetable is ready to be picked
is only part of harvesting successfully. Equally important is the
length of time each vegetable can retain its fresh taste from harvest to table. Some, like sprouts and summer squash, should be
used as soon after they have been picked as possible. Others, like
garlic, onions and winter squash, can be stored for long periods of
time. Unless you are going to eat the entire crop right away, you
will want to know the best methods for storing the remainder.

On the following pages you will find specific harvesting and storage techniques that can extend the pleasures of your
summer vegetable garden into the fall and winter. You will
discover how to recognize, and how to accelerate, different kinds
of ripeness. You will also learn how to pick, cure and keep vegetables so that they look and taste good long after their season
of ripening is only a warm memory.

RETRIEVING POTATOES FROM UNDERGROUND

Tender-skinned and sweet-flavored, these new potatoes have been unearthed while still attached to the plant's underground stem system. Digging up new potatoes will not harm the plant or interfere with an abundant fall harvest; tubers will continue to form on the remaining underground stems.

There are many reasons to grow potatoes. They take up little space in your garden, they can be harvested through much of the summer, they store well and they taste better than the ones you buy. Despite appearances, the potato is not a root but a tuber, an underground stem swollen with nutrients. The plant concentrates all its goodness in the tuber; the green parts of the potato plant—seeds, leaves, fruit and aboveground stems—are poisonous.

The small, thin-skinned potatoes called new potatoes are actually immature potatoes. You can gather them seven or eight weeks after planting; picking some will not harm the crop. The plants will be leafy and green; to be sure the potatoes are ready for eating, reach into the soil below the foliage, feel around for some boiling-size potatoes and detach them from their roots. Don't try to store these early pickings; eat them at once for their tender texture and delicate flavor.

When the plants turn brown and start to die, the potatoes are no longer new. They can be harvested as full-grown potatoes any time from then until the first frost. But be sure to dig them before the first frost; they cannot withstand the cold. Remove them one by one from the soil or raise several at once with a rounded potato rake *(opposite)* or with a garden fork. Choose a time when you have had a few days of dry weather so the plants and the soil will not be waterlogged.

With proper care, potatoes can be stored all winter. Do not wash them. Store only potatoes that have no cuts or bruises, which beget infection. Before storing, cure the potatoes for two weeks in a dark, humid room at 50° to 60° F. Then move them to a dark, dry, cool, well-ventilated place, like a basement. To prevent sprouting, keep stored potatoes away from light and make sure the temperature remains below 50° F.

Potatoes will suffocate in airtight containers; store them in wooden barrels, crates or bushel baskets, or in metal or plastic garbage cans with holes punched in the sides and bottom. You can even pile potatoes loosely in a corner, as long as it is dark, dry and cool.

1 When the foliage of potato plants turns brown, thrust a potato rake into the hill beneath the plants and gently pull up the potatoes *(left)*. If the ground has hardened, carefully break up the surface with the rake, loosen the soil around the plants, then dig underneath to lift out potatoes. Shake off loose soil but do not wash the potatoes. Leaving potatoes in the ground over the winter invites disease that can harm next year's crop; feel around in the hill with your hand to make sure you have got them all.

2 Spread unearthed potatoes on the ground for one or two days to dry out and harden their skins. The tougher the skin, the longer a potato can be stored without loss of flavor. Any attached stems will break away as the potatoes dry. Store only unblemished potatoes, and eat the rest as soon as possible. □

PICKING SQUASH AND STORING IT

All members of the squash family are planted the same way; you can sow seeds indoors *(pages 24-25)* or outdoors *(pages 32-35)*. Many grow on vines and show other marks of kinship. But when it comes to harvesting, the family breaks into a pair of distinct branches. Summer squashes, as the name implies, should be picked during the warm months, when they are dewy fresh and their skins are tender. In fact, zucchini and the tubular yellow varieties taste best when only about 6 inches long, and disc-shaped scallop squash should be picked early, too. After picking, any of these can be stored in a refrigerator, but only for about a week.

The winter squashes are an entirely different matter. Acorn squash, Hubbards, butternuts, turban and spaghetti squash, and pumpkins—which are really just large squash—can all be stored without refrigeration for months and make excellent eating through the winter. If harvested when young, they will be watery inside and lack sweetness. Instead, they should be allowed to mature on the vine as long as possible —almost until the first hard frost. Partly because they take so long to mature, they need special treatment *(opposite)* at harvest time, and after picking as well.

All winter squashes need to be cured for a few weeks in a dark, warm, well-ventilated room to dry and harden their skins. In the basement, near the furnace will do, with perhaps a house fan turned on to help circulate the air.

After curing, squashes should be stored in a single layer—again for ventilation— on open shelves in a dry place that stays about 50° or 55° F all winter. A garage might do, or a closet in a spare room where the heat is not turned up. Preserved in this way, acorns and Hubbards and turbans remain deliciously fresh into the dark months, and pumpkins can provide pies long after Thanksgiving and even Christmas are past.

Resting on thin boards so that they will grow round and full, small pumpkins turn orange in the slanted autumn sunlight as they ripen for picking.

1 When winter squash and pumpkins *(left)* approach full development in late summer, place them on small boards or shingles. Off the ground, they will stay dry and free of rot. Roll them a quarter turn once a week so that they will be evenly colored and will not develop a flat side.

2 To test whether a squash or a pumpkin is ready for picking, try to pierce the skin with your thumbnail. If the skin breaks, the pumpkin is unripe (but don't worry; the wound will heal). If it is impervious to your nail, the vegetable is ready to pick.

3 To harvest squash or pumpkins, cut them off the vine, leaving 3 inches of stem attached. Do not carry any of these vegetables by its stem; the weight will weaken the connection and the vegetable will spoil. If you do break off a stem, eat that squash first, since it will not keep well.

4 After picking, you can leave squash outside for a day if the weather is sunny and there is no threat of frost. This will begin the curing process that hardens the skin. The sun will also dry any clinging dirt, which can be brushed off with your hand. Never wash a winter squash or a pumpkin except just before cooking; water removes a natural preservative coating from the skin and the vegetable will spoil quickly. □

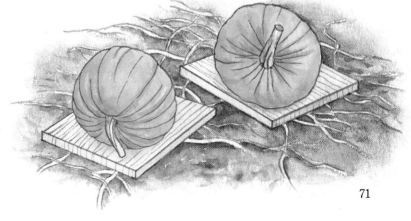

VEGETABLE SPROUTS— READY TO EAT IN A WEEK

Almost everyone knows about bean sprouts, thanks to the prevalence of Oriental cooking. Less well known is the fact that many other seeds can also be sprouted, for use in salads and cooking. Along with the familiar mung beans and soybeans, you can sprout snap beans, lentils, peas and chickpeas. The seeds of radish, broccoli, cabbage, celery, cauliflower and cress produce delicious sprouts, each with its own distinctive texture and taste. Some are crisp, some soft, some nutty, some sweet, some piquant.

In choosing seeds for sprouting, there are a few caveats. Avoid the seeds of plants whose foliage is known to be toxic, such as rhubarb and tomato. Also, look for seeds that have not been treated with chemical preservatives, a common practice in commercial seed houses. Some seed houses specialize in untreated seeds (check the seed packets for this information), and health food stores are also a good source.

The procedures for sprouting seeds could scarcely be simpler. All they need is moisture, gentle warmth and enough air circulation to prevent mold from forming. Customarily the sprouts are grown in bowls or wide-mouthed Mason jars covered with netting or cheesecloth, and must be rinsed twice a day to keep the sprouts from souring. But in the method shown here, especially recommended for small seeds, the sprouts are grown in the open air, on trays fitted with moist paper toweling. As the seeds germinate, their tiny, filament-like roots anchor in the toweling and the sprouts grow straight up instead of in a tangled mass. They can be harvested simply with a pair of scissors *(opposite)*.

A glass dish overflows with alfalfa sprouts that are about one week old. Alfalfa and many other vegetables (left) can be made to sprout in any season—and need no soil.

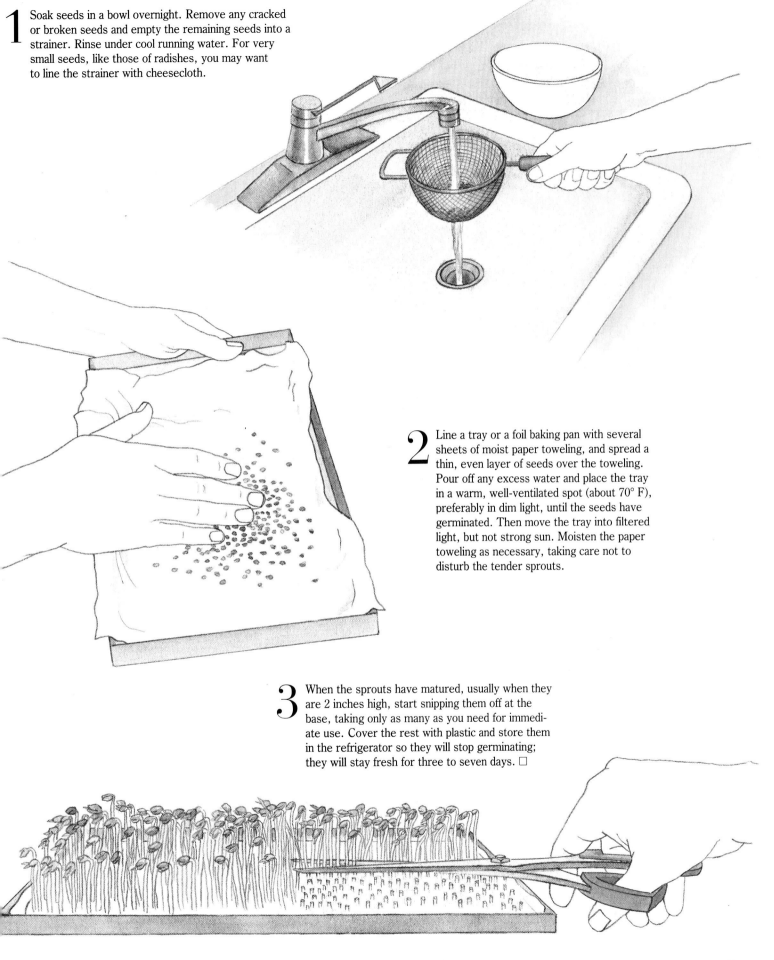

1 Soak seeds in a bowl overnight. Remove any cracked or broken seeds and empty the remaining seeds into a strainer. Rinse under cool running water. For very small seeds, like those of radishes, you may want to line the strainer with cheesecloth.

2 Line a tray or a foil baking pan with several sheets of moist paper toweling, and spread a thin, even layer of seeds over the toweling. Pour off any excess water and place the tray in a warm, well-ventilated spot (about 70° F), preferably in dim light, until the seeds have germinated. Then move the tray into filtered light, but not strong sun. Moisten the paper toweling as necessary, taking care not to disturb the tender sprouts.

3 When the sprouts have matured, usually when they are 2 inches high, start snipping them off at the base, taking only as many as you need for immediate use. Cover the rest with plastic and store them in the refrigerator so they will stop germinating; they will stay fresh for three to seven days. □

BRAIDING ONIONS AND GARLIC FOR STORAGE

Braids of white garlic, nut-brown shallots and plump yellow onions hang in winter storage. Supported by their own intertwined stems, the aromatic bulbs will remain edible for up to a year.

You can savor the pungency of homegrown onions and garlic bulbs all winter long if you harvest, cure and store them under the proper conditions. The plants themselves will tell you when to harvest. With onions, wait until the gray-green stalks begin to turn brown and droop to the ground. This is a sign that the bulbs have matured. If all but a few of the stalks are down, the remainder can be pushed over to hasten the ripening of the slower-maturing bulbs.

After a week, pull up all the onion plants, being careful not to break the stalks from the bulbs. Pull up garlic plants when their lower stems and leaves start turning yellow.

Both onion and garlic bulbs must be dried slightly before long-term storage so their skins toughen, or cure. If the weather is dry and sunny, lay the newly pulled plants on the ground; if the soil surface feels damp or if you expect rain, take the plants indoors and spread them on sheets of newspaper.

After curing, onions and garlic can be packed in wooden crates or baskets (no more than two layers deep), suspended in mesh bags or twisted into braids for hanging. Braiding not only makes the bulbs look attractive, it also provides maximum protection against rot during storage, since it allows each bulb exposure to circulating air.

When you braid *(opposite),* start out with three strands; then add strands to the outside edges of the braid one at a time, alternating between the left outer edge and the right outer edge. The last strand to be added to the braid is always crossed over into the center of the braid.

Hang the completed braids up to dry in a warm place (70° to 80° F) for three weeks. Then transfer them to a cool, dry, well-ventilated place like a cellar, a covered porch or an unheated spare room. For onions, storage at a temperature of 32° to 45° F is preferable; garlic does best at 50° F.

To remove an individual bulb as needed, carefully cut or twist it off its stem without disturbing the rest of the braid.

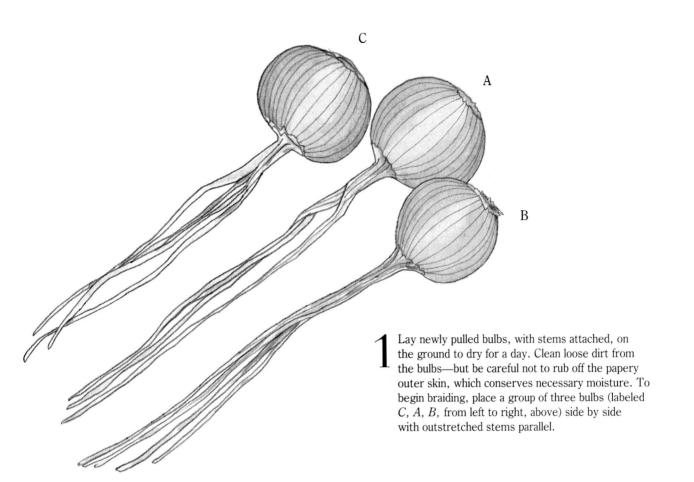

1 Lay newly pulled bulbs, with stems attached, on the ground to dry for a day. Clean loose dirt from the bulbs—but be careful not to rub off the papery outer skin, which conserves necessary moisture. To begin braiding, place a group of three bulbs (labeled *C, A, B,* from left to right, above) side by side with outstretched stems parallel.

2 Take hold of the stem of the bulb on the right (labeled *B)* with your thumb and forefinger, and lay it on top of the stem of the middle bulb (labeled *A).*

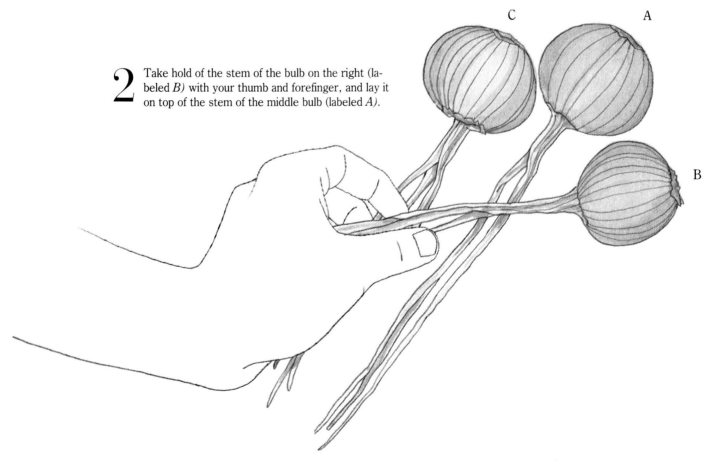

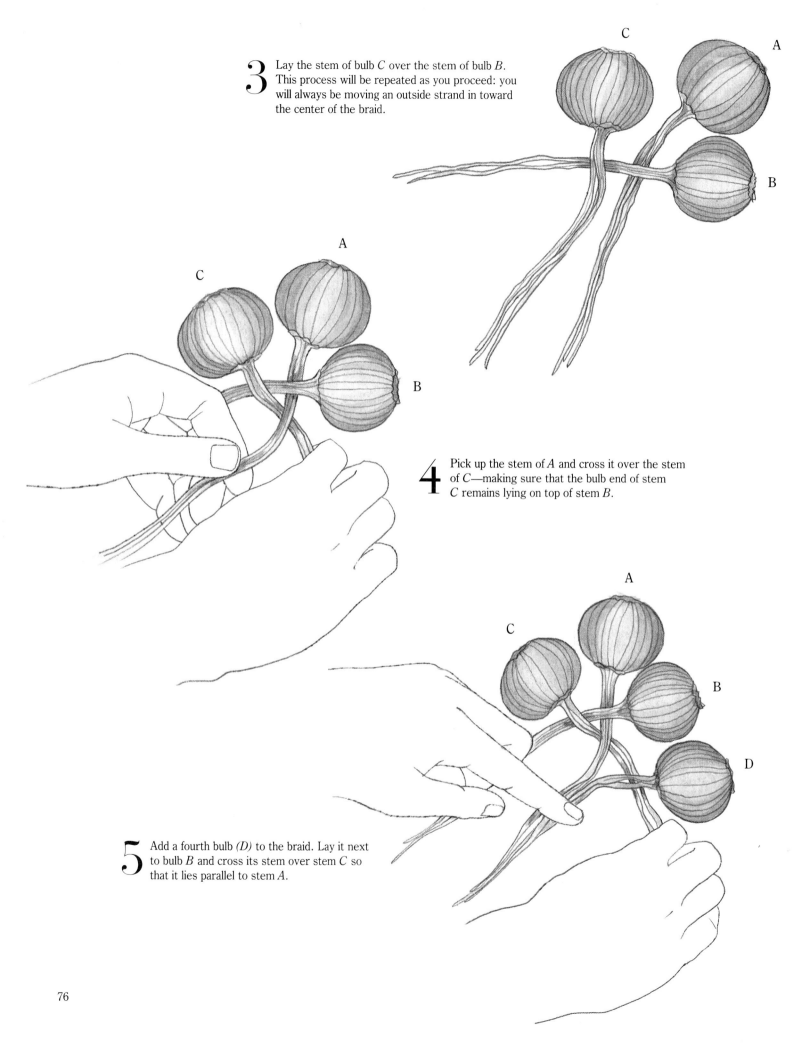

3 Lay the stem of bulb *C* over the stem of bulb *B*. This process will be repeated as you proceed: you will always be moving an outside strand in toward the center of the braid.

4 Pick up the stem of *A* and cross it over the stem of *C*—making sure that the bulb end of stem *C* remains lying on top of stem *B*.

5 Add a fourth bulb *(D)* to the braid. Lay it next to bulb *B* and cross its stem over stem *C* so that it lies parallel to stem *A*.

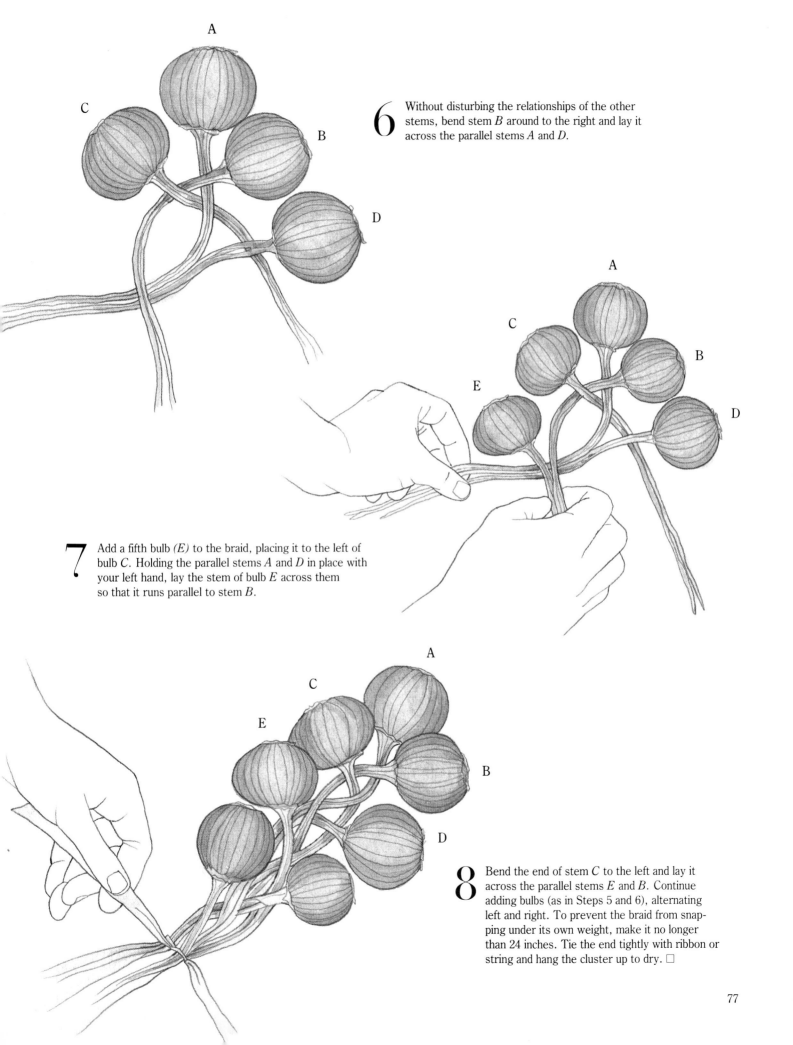

6 Without disturbing the relationships of the other stems, bend stem *B* around to the right and lay it across the parallel stems *A* and *D*.

7 Add a fifth bulb *(E)* to the braid, placing it to the left of bulb *C*. Holding the parallel stems *A* and *D* in place with your left hand, lay the stem of bulb *E* across them so that it runs parallel to stem *B*.

8 Bend the end of stem *C* to the left and lay it across the parallel stems *E* and *B*. Continue adding bulbs (as in Steps 5 and 6), alternating left and right. To prevent the braid from snapping under its own weight, make it no longer than 24 inches. Tie the end tightly with ribbon or string and hang the cluster up to dry. □

5
MAKING THE MOST OF NATURE

Along with good soil, good seeds and good care, a successful vegetable garden depends on good timing. Because some seeds must stay cool to germinate and some seedlings shrink from the slightest hint of frost, your decisions about when to plant which crops will be critical in determining the size of your harvest. To help you plan ahead, the map on pages 80-81 shows the average date of the last frost in nine different regions across the United States and Canada. For more specific guidance, turn to the table of region-by-region, crop-by-crop planting dates starting on page 82.

In the battle against garden pests, victory goes to those who know their enemy. The knowledge you need to fight back can be found on pages 86-89. Entries are arranged to help you identify a common problem, pinpoint the cause and take effective action.

In addition, there are tips on how to take advantage of the natural insect-repelling properties of crops like garlic and radishes—and how to cultivate common vegetables like asparagus and eggplant for their beauty as well as their taste. Also included are tips and techniques for improving soil, raising blanched vegetables, speeding up seeds, getting big harvests out of small spaces and introducing your children to the many pleasures of gardening.

SPRING FROST DATES

Success with a summer vegetable garden—more than almost any other kind of garden—depends on choosing the proper planting date. Timing is critical, because each crop needs the right soil temperature to get off to a strong start. Some vegetables, even though they grow and mature in the summer, need cool soil to germinate and must therefore be planted a few weeks before the last spring frost; others need warm soil and cannot safely be planted until after all danger of frost has passed.

The map at right is a guide to determining planting dates. It is based on average last frost dates compiled over a 30-year period by the Department of Commerce, and divides North America into nine regions. Region 1, primarily Canada and the northernmost areas of the United States, has the longest winter and may have frost as late as mid-June. Region 9, which includes the southern areas of California, Florida and Texas, is free of frost as early as January 30—and in fact some parts of the region may never experience frost at all.

The regions on the map and the dates that go with them are meant to be used as general guidelines only. In certain years temperatures may be higher or lower than usual and planting dates may have to be adjusted accordingly. Check with your local agricultural extension service for information specific to your area and to the year in which you are planting.

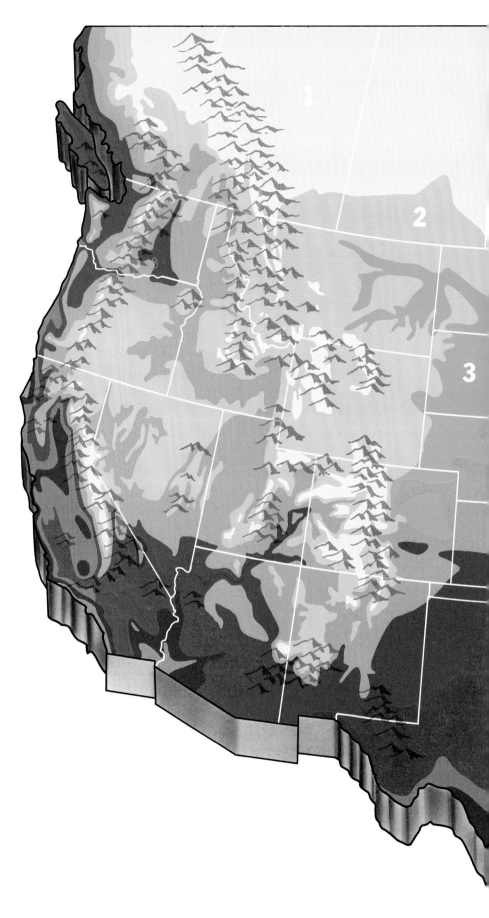

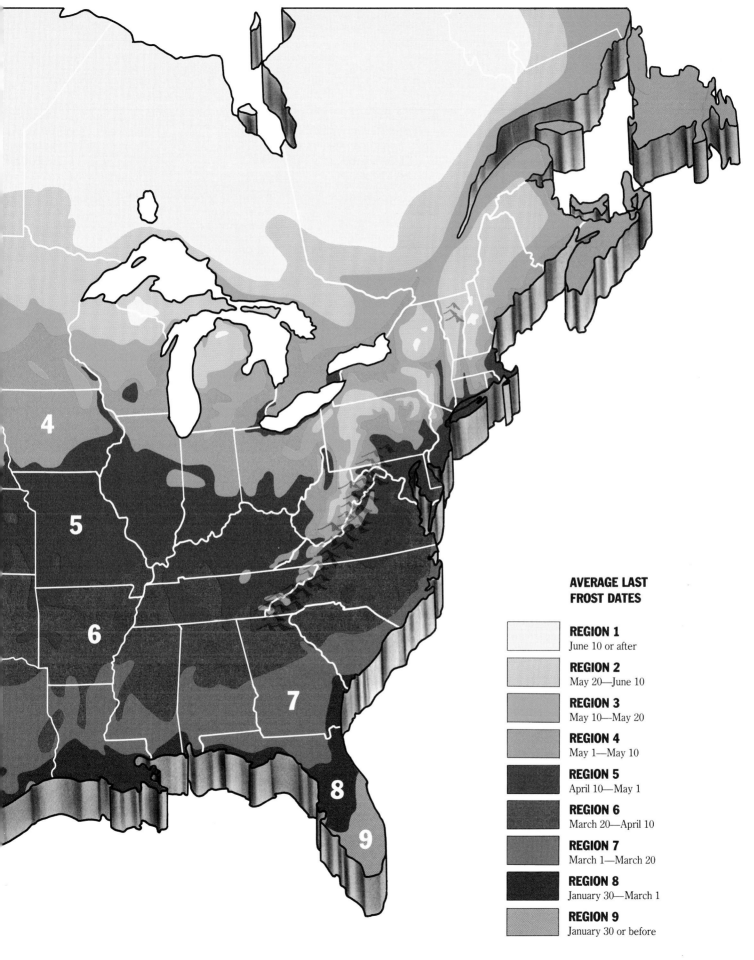

**AVERAGE LAST
FROST DATES**

REGION 1
June 10 or after

REGION 2
May 20—June 10

REGION 3
May 10—May 20

REGION 4
May 1—May 10

REGION 5
April 10—May 1

REGION 6
March 20—April 10

REGION 7
March 1—March 20

REGION 8
January 30—March 1

REGION 9
January 30 or before

PLANTING DATES
FOR SUMMER VEGETABLES

		REGION 1	REGION 2	REGION 3	REGION 4
ARTICHOKE	Seeds and roots	Not recommended	Not recommended	Not recommended	May 10–May 30
ASPARAGUS	Roots	May 15–June 10	May 1–June 1	Apr. 20–May 15	Mar. 30–Apr. 30
BEET	Seeds	May 15–June 15	May 1–June 15	Apr. 25–June 15	Apr. 15–July 15
CARROT	Seeds	May 20–June 15	May 10–June 15	May 1–July 1	Apr. 20–July 10
CELERIAC AND CELERY	Seedlings	June 1–June 15	May 20–June 15	May 10–July 1	Apr. 20–July 5
CHICORY	Seeds	May 30–June 15	May 15–June 15	May 15–June 15	June 1–July 1
CORN	Seeds	Not recommended	May 20–June 10	May 15–June 15	May 5–June 15
CUCUMBER	Seeds	Not recommended	Not recommended	June 1–June 15	May 20–July 1
DRY BEANS	Seeds	Not recommended	May 25–June 15	May 15–June 30	May 10–July 10
EGGPLANT	Seedlings	Not recommended	Not recommended	June 1–June 15	May 20–June 15
GARBANZO BEANS	Seeds	Not recommended	May 25–June 15	May 15–June 30	May 10–July 10
GARLIC	Cloves	May 15–June 1	May 1–May 30	Apr. 15–May 15	Apr. 1–May 1
HORSERADISH	Roots	May 15–June 1	May 1–May 30	Apr. 20–May 20	Apr. 15–May 15
HORTICULTURAL BEANS	Seeds	Not recommended	June 10–July 1	May 30–July 1	May 25–July 15
JERUSALEM ARTICHOKE	Tubers	Not recommended	Not recommended	May 20–June 20	May 10–June 30
LEEKS	Seeds	May 1–June 1	May 1–June 1	May 1–May 20	Apr. 15–May 15
LETTUCE (HEAD)	Seedlings	May 20–June 30	May 10–June 30	May 1–July 15	Apr. 15–May 15 June 15–Aug. 1
LETTUCE (LEAF)	Seeds and seedlings	May 20–July 15	May 10–July 15	May 1–Aug. 1	Apr. 15–Aug. 1
LIMA BEANS	Seeds	Not recommended	Not recommended	Not recommended	May 25–June 15
OKRA	Seeds	Not recommended	Not recommended	June 1–June 20	May 20–July 1
ONION	Seedlings	May 1–June 10	May 1–May 30	Apr. 20–May 15	Apr. 10–May 1

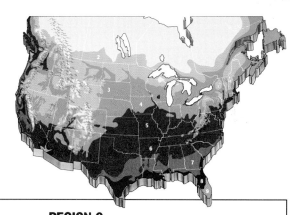

REGION 5	REGION 6	REGION 7	REGION 8	REGION 9	
Apr. 30–May 30	Apr. 10–May 30	Mar. 20–Apr. 30	Feb. 28–Apr. 30	Jan. 30–Apr. 30 Jan. 1 in frost-free areas	ARTICHOKE
Mar. 15–Apr. 15	Feb. 15–Apr. 10	Dec. 1–Mar. 10	Dec. 1–Feb. 28 Certain varieties only; see Dictionary	Dec. 1–Feb. 1 Certain varieties only; see Dictionary	ASPARAGUS
Mar. 20–Aug. 15	Mar. 1–Sept. 1	Feb. 15–Oct. 1	Jan. 10–Dec. 1	Jan. 10–Dec. 1	BEET
Apr. 1–Aug. 1	Mar. 1–Apr. 20 July 15–Aug. 15	Feb. 10–Mar. 20 Aug. 15–Sept. 1	Jan. 10–Mar. 1 Sept. 1–Dec. 1	Jan. 10–Mar. 1 Sept. 15–Dec. 1	CARROT
Apr. 10–June 15	Mar. 15–May 30	Feb. 20–Apr. 1	Jan. 10–Mar. 1	Sept. 1–Feb. 1	CELERIAC AND CELERY
June 15–July 15	June 1–July 1	June 1–July 1	Sept. 1–Oct. 1	Sept. 15–Oct. 15	CHICORY
Apr. 25–June 1	Mar. 25–June 1	Mar. 15–May 1	Feb. 10–Apr. 15	Feb. 1–Mar. 15	CORN
May 1–July 15	Apr. 10–Aug. 1	Mar. 20–May 1 June 1–Aug. 15	Feb. 15–Apr. 15 June 1–Sept. 15	Feb. 15–Mar. 15 Aug. 15–Oct. 1	CUCUMBER
Apr. 25–Aug. 1	Apr. 1–Aug. 15	Mar. 15–Sept. 1	Feb. 1–Sept. 20	Feb. 1–Nov. 1	DRY BEANS
May 10–July 1	Apr. 15–July 1	Mar. 25–July 15	Mar. 1–Sept. 1	Feb. 1–Sept. 30	EGGPLANT
Apr. 25–Aug. 1	Apr. 1–Aug. 15	Mar. 15–Sept. 1	Feb. 1–Sept. 20	Feb. 1–Nov. 1	GARBANZO BEANS
Mar. 10–Apr. 15	Feb. 10–Mar. 20	Feb. 1–Mar. 1 Aug. 1–Oct. 1	Aug. 15–Nov. 15	Sept. 15–Nov. 15	GARLIC
Mar. 20–Apr. 30	Mar. 1–Apr. 10	Aug. 30–Oct. 30	Sept. 15–Nov. 25	Oct. 1–Dec. 15	HORSERADISH
May 10–July 15	Apr. 15–July 25	Mar. 25–July 25	Mar. 1–July 25	Feb. 15–July 25	HORTICULTURAL BEANS
Apr. 30–July 10	Apr. 10–July 10	Mar. 20–July 10	Feb. 28–July 10	Jan. 1–July 10	JERUSALEM ARTICHOKE
Mar. 15–May 1	Feb. 15–Apr. 1	Jan. 25–Mar. 15	Jan. 1–Mar. 1	Jan. 1–Feb. 15	LEEKS
Mar. 20–May 1 July 15–Aug. 30	Mar. 1–Apr. 1 Aug. 1–Sept. 15	Feb. 1–Mar. 10 Aug. 15–Oct. 15	Jan. 1–Feb. 15 Sept. 1–Dec. 1	Sept. 15–Feb. 1	LETTUCE (HEAD)
Mar. 20–June 1 July 15–Sept. 1	Feb. 15–Mar. 15 Aug. 15–Oct. 1	Jan. 15–Apr. 1 Aug. 25–Oct. 1	Jan. 1–Mar. 15 Sept. 1–Dec. 1	Sept. 15–Feb. 1	LETTUCE (LEAF)
May 1–June 30	Apr. 1–Aug. 1	Mar. 20–Aug. 15	Feb. 10–Sept. 15	Feb. 1–Oct. 1	LIMA BEANS
May 1–Aug. 1	Apr. 10–Aug. 10	Mar. 20–Aug. 20	Mar. 1–Sept. 20	Feb. 15–Oct. 1	OKRA
Mar. 15–May 1	Feb. 15–Apr. 1	Jan. 15–Mar. 10	Oct. 1–Feb. 1	Oct. 1–Jan. 15	ONION

		REGION 1	**REGION 2**	**REGION 3**	**REGION 4**
ONION	Seeds	May 1–June 10	May 1–May 30	Apr. 20–May 15	Apr. 1–May 1
ONION	Sets	May 1–June 10	May 1–May 30	Apr. 20–May 15	Apr. 10–May 1
PARSNIPS	Seeds	May 20–June 10	May 10–June 15	May 1–June 15	Apr. 15–July 1
PEPPERS	Seedlings	Not recommended	June 10–June 20	May 25–June 20	May 20–July 1
POTATO	Tubers	May 5–June 1	Apr. 30–June 1	Apr. 15–June 10	Apr. 1–June 10
PUMPKIN	Seeds	Not recommended	Not recommended	May 20–June 10	June 1–June 15
RHUBARB	Roots	May 15–June 1	May 1–May 20	Apr. 15–May 10	Apr. 1–May 1
SALSIFY	Seeds	May 25–June 1	May 10–June 10	May 1–June 20	Apr. 15–June 20
SHALLOT	Cloves	May 20–June 10	May 1–June 10	Apr. 20–May 20	Apr. 10–May 1
SNAP BEANS	Seeds	Not recommended	May 25–June 15	May 15–June 30	May 10–July 10
SORREL	Seeds	May 20–June 15	May 1–June 15	May 1–July 1	Apr. 15–July 15
SOUTHERN PEAS	Seeds	Not recommended	Not recommended	Not recommended	Not recommended
SOYBEANS	Seeds	Not recommended	Not recommended	Not recommended	May 25–June 10
SUMMER SPINACH	Seeds	Not recommended	June 10–June 20	May 20–July 1	May 10–July 1
SUMMER SQUASH	Seeds and seedlings	June 10–June 20	June 10–June 20	May 20–July 1	May 10–July 1
SWEET POTATO	Slips	Not recommended	Not recommended	Not recommended	Not recommended
SWISS CHARD	Seeds	May 30–June 15	May 10–June 30	May 1–July 1	Apr. 20–July 5
TAMPALA	Seeds	June 10–June 30	June 10–July 10	May 20–July 20	May 10–July 30
TOMATILLO AND TOMATO	Seedlings	June 15–June 30	June 10–June 30	May 25–June 30	May 15–June 30
WATERCRESS	Seeds	Not recommended	May 20–Aug. 15	May 10–Aug. 15	May 1–Aug. 30
WINTER SQUASH	Seeds and seedlings	Not recommended	Not recommended	May 20–June 10	June 1–June 15

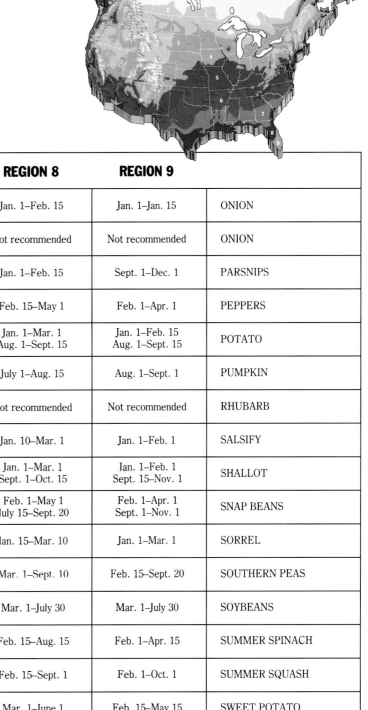

REGION 5	REGION 6	REGION 7	REGION 8	REGION 9	
Mar. 15–Apr. 15	Feb. 20–Apr. 1	Feb. 1–Mar. 10	Jan. 1–Feb. 15	Jan. 1–Jan. 15	ONION
Mar. 10–Apr. 10	Feb. 15–Apr. 1	Not recommended	Not recommended	Not recommended	ONION
Mar. 20–July 10	Mar. 1–Apr. 10	Jan. 15–Mar. 15	Jan. 1–Feb. 15	Sept. 1–Dec. 1	PARSNIPS
May 10–July 10	Apr. 15–July 20	Apr. 1–Aug. 1	Feb. 15–May 1	Feb. 1–Apr. 1	PEPPERS
Mar. 15–June 1	Feb. 20–Apr. 15	Feb. 1–Mar. 15 July 25–Aug. 20	Jan. 1–Mar. 1 Aug. 1–Sept. 15	Jan. 1–Feb. 15 Aug. 1–Sept. 15	POTATO
May 15–July 1	May 30–July 10	June 15–July 20	July 1–Aug. 15	Aug. 1–Sept. 1	PUMPKIN
Mar. 10–Apr. 15	Mar. 1–Apr. 1	Not recommended	Not recommended	Not recommended	RHUBARB
Mar. 20–July 1	Mar. 1–July 10	Feb. 1–June 15	Jan. 10–Mar. 1	Jan. 1–Feb. 1	SALSIFY
Mar. 15–May 1	Feb. 15–Apr. 10	Jan. 15–Mar. 20 Aug. 15–Oct. 1	Jan. 1–Mar. 1 Sept. 1–Oct. 15	Jan. 1–Feb. 1 Sept. 15–Nov. 1	SHALLOT
Apr. 25–Aug. 1	Apr. 1–Aug. 15	Mar. 15–May 15 July 1–Sept. 1	Feb. 1–May 1 July 15–Sept. 20	Feb. 1–Apr. 1 Sept. 1–Nov. 1	SNAP BEANS
Mar. 15–May 15	Feb. 20–Apr. 15	Feb. 10–Mar. 20	Jan. 15–Mar. 10	Jan. 1–Mar. 1	SORREL
May 10 July 1	Apr. 15–Aug. 1	Mar. 25–Sept. 1	Mar. 1–Sept. 10	Feb. 15–Sept. 20	SOUTHERN PEAS
May 10–June 25	Apr. 20–July 15	Apr. 10–July 25	Mar. 1–July 30	Mar. 1–July 30	SOYBEANS
May 1–Aug. 1	Apr. 10–Aug. 1	Mar. 20–Aug. 15	Feb. 15–Aug. 15	Feb. 1–Apr. 15	SUMMER SPINACH
May 1–July 20	Apr. 10–Aug. 1	Mar. 15–Aug. 10	Feb. 15–Sept. 1	Feb. 1–Oct. 1	SUMMER SQUASH
May 10–June 10	Apr. 20–June 15	Apr. 1–June 1	Mar. 1–June 1	Feb. 15–May 15	SWEET POTATO
Apr. 1–Aug. 1	Mar. 1–Sept. 10	Feb. 15–Sept. 1	Jan. 10–Oct. 1	Jan. 1–Nov. 1	SWISS CHARD
Apr. 30–Aug. 1	Apr. 10–Aug. 15	Mar. 20–Sept. 1	Feb. 28–Sept. 1	Jan. 1–Oct. 1	TAMPALA
May 5–July 1	Apr. 10–June 1	Mar. 20–May 20	Feb. 28–May 1	Feb. 1–Apr. 1	TOMATILLO AND TOMATO
Apr. 10–Sept. 15	Mar. 20–Sept. 30	Mar. 1–Oct. 15	Jan. 30–Nov. 1	All year	WATERCRESS
June 1–July 1	June 10–July 10	June 20–July 20	July 1–Aug. 15	Aug. 1–Sept. 1	WINTER SQUASH

WHAT TO DO
WHEN THINGS GO WRONG

PROBLEM	CAUSE	SOLUTION
Brown spots ringed with yellow appear on leaves of tomatoes or potatoes. Tomatoes may rot at the stem end and have dark, leathery, sunken spots that can spread over the rest of the fruit. Potatoes will develop brown, corky, dry spots. Yields are sometimes reduced.	Early blight, caused by the fungus *Alternaria.* Called early blight because it occurs in the spring. *(See late blight, below.)*	Rotate crops and destroy infected plants at the end of the season. Treat with a fungicide safe for vegetables. When planting seed potatoes, use only those certified disease-free by the state agricultural department.
Dark, irregular spots appear on leaves of tomatoes and potatoes, and there may be a white mold on the lower leaf surface. Fruits and tubers can also be affected with darkened, rotting spots.	Late blight, caused by the fungus *Phytophthora.* Called late blight because it occurs in fall.	Treat with a fungicide recommended for vegetables. Rotate crops and destroy all infected plants in fall. When planting seed potatoes, use only those certified disease-free.
Brown pockmarks form on bean pods; sunken spots with rings develop on ripe tomatoes.	Anthracnose, a fungus disease.	Keep the garden free of weeds and debris. Rotate crops every three years. Spray with sulfur, starting in early spring, or with a fungicide recommended for vegetables.
Seeds rot in the soil or young seedlings suddenly wilt, fall over and die.	Damping-off, a fungus disease. Any vegetable can be affected.	Use a sterile, soilless medium to start seeds indoors, and do not overwater flats. Make sure the garden soil has good drainage. Use treated seeds or treat the medium with a recommended fungicide. Do not plant outdoors if soil is too damp or too cold.
White dust develops on the lower surfaces of leaves and spreads over the entire leaf and stem, causing distortion on beans, cucumbers, squash and pumpkins.	Powdery mildew, a fungus disease.	Space plants so air can circulate between them. Thin seedlings to avoid crowding. Do not water late in the day; cool night air and damp soil foster spread of disease. Spray with sulfur when temperature is below 85° F or treat with a fungicide safe for vegetables.
Vegetable foliage, especially that of rhubarb, develops tiny yellow spots that later turn brown, enlarge and have red margins.	Leaf spot, a fungus disease.	Treat with a recommended fungicide, beginning in spring when growth starts. Do not water late in the day. Remove all foliage and debris from the garden in fall.
Foliage of beans, cucumbers, squash, pumpkins or peppers becomes mottled, yellowed or curled. Fruits may be discolored or streaked.	Mosaic, a virus disease.	Plant varieties resistant to mosaic virus. As the virus is spread by aphids, control these insects and remove all weeds where they may live and breed.

PROBLEM	CAUSE	SOLUTION
Tiny white or green growths, or galls, form on corn ears, stalks and tassels, usually at the top of the plant. At maturity, the galls turn black and burst open, releasing large numbers of black powdery spores.	Smut, a fungus disease.	There are no chemical controls for smut. Remove the galls before they burst open. Rotate crops and plant resistant varieties.
Edges of lettuce leaves darken and appear to be burned.	Tip burn, a condition caused by high heat, lack of calcium and uneven soil moisture.	Grow lettuce in moist soil in a partially shaded location during the heat of summer.
Sunken pockmarks with black mold form on cucumbers, squash and pumpkins; plants and fruits may be distorted. Rough, corky scabs appear on potatoes.	Scab, a bacterial or fungus disease.	Rotate crops. Plant seeds that are disease-free and varieties that are resistant to scab and seed potatoes that are certified resistant to scab. There is no chemical cure for bacterial scab, which affects potatoes, but a soil pH under 5.5 will prevent the disease. Cucumbers, squash and pumpkins may be treated with a recommended fungicide.
Sunken, dry areas develop on onions just before harvest or while they are in storage. A crusty layer of hard black tissue forms around the neck, and gray, moldy growth forms between the inside layers.	Neck rot, a fungus disease.	There are no chemical controls for neck rot. Do not harvest bulbs until the tops brown and fall over, and dry the bulbs completely before storing them.
Both sides of leaves on asparagus and bean plants develop small, rust-colored spots; then they turn yellow and drop.	Rust, a fungus disease.	Water early in the day to prevent disease spread on wet leaves. Dust or spray with sulfur when the temperature is below 85° F or use a fungicide safe for vegetables. Destroy infected plants in fall.
Brown cracks and lesions appear on the inner and outer surfaces of celery stalks.	Brown check, which is caused by a boron deficiency.	Add 2 ounces of borax to every 30 pounds of fertilizer before applying it to celery, or make a dilute borax solution and apply it to the base of the plant.
Vine crops such as cucumbers, squash and pumpkins suddenly wilt and die. Leaves may turn brown before wilting. Seedlings of these vine crops, tomatoes and eggplant are stunted, and eventually wilt and die.	Wilt caused by bacteria or by *Fusarium* or *Verticillium* fungus. A cross-section of the affected plant's stem will show brown streaks.	Bacterial wilt spreads by cucumber beetles, which must be controlled. To control fusarium and verticillium wilt in tomatoes, plant only resistant varieties. Fusarium wilt does not affect eggplant; there are no verticillium-resistant varieties of eggplant. Remove any diseased plants immediately and clean up the garden completely in the fall. Rotate crops. Acid soil will deter these fungi.
Blossom ends of tomatoes have sunken, tough, black patches.	Blossom-end rot, caused by a calcium deficiency brought about by uneven moisture levels in the soil.	Make sure that the garden receives an inch of water per week. Mulch to retain moisture in the soil during dry periods. Have your soil pH checked to make sure it is between 5.5 and 7.0; this pH level makes calcium soluble.

PROBLEM	CAUSE	SOLUTION
Small holes in the leaves, flowers and fruit of many vegetables. Eventually, plants may be stripped of all foliage.	Beetles, including asparagus, flea, cucumber, Colorado potato, Mexican bean and Japanese beetles, ¼- to ½-inch insects with hard shells.	Hand-pick larger beetles from the plant. Control larvae with milky spore, a bacterium fatal to beetles but harmless to plants and other animals. Keep the garden weeded; beetles lay eggs in weedy areas. Spray with a pesticide recommended for vegetables.
Leaves of plants are withered, curled or distorted; ants appear on stems and leaves. Any vegetable can be affected.	Aphids, ⅛-inch insects, of various colors, that suck plant juices and secrete a sticky substance that can spread disease and attract ants.	Aphids can be washed off with a heavy stream of water or destroyed with a pesticide spray recommended for vegetables.
Vine crops wilt, dry out and turn black. Leaf tips and stem joints of beans, beets, Swiss chard, celery or potato plants are deformed and turn black.	Plant bugs, especially the ¼-inch tarnished plant bug or the ⅝-inch squash bug.	Hand-pick the bugs and remove damaged leaves. Apply an insecticide that is recommended for vegetables. Remove all infested plants in fall.
Plants, especially young transplants, are eaten or cut off at the base at soil level.	Cutworms, gray, brown or black caterpillars up to 2 inches long.	Make a protective collar out of a milk container, a can or a paper cup and place it around young seedlings. Wood ashes around the base of the plant are a deterrent. Remove infested plants in fall.
Corn kernels are eaten within the husk. Insides of tomatoes are eaten away.	Corn earworm (also known as tomato fruitworm), a 1- to 2-inch caterpillar with lengthwise stripes.	Spray with a pesticide recommended for vegetables. Remove and destroy all infested plants in fall.
Large holes are eaten in leaves; ripe fruits are destroyed; seedlings may be eaten. Tomatoes are especially susceptible. Silver streaks appear on leaves and garden paths.	Snails or slugs (shell-less snails), night-feeding pests up to 3 inches long.	Trap slugs in saucers of beer or grapefruit halves turned upside down. Salt kills snails and slugs, but may damage crops. Bait is available; choose one safe for vegetables.
Plants wilt on warm days or become stunted, light in color or low in yield. Roots are swollen and knotted. Any summer vegetable except corn and beans may be affected.	Nematodes, eelworms too small to be visible to the eye; only a soil test will confirm their presence.	Rotate crops or relocate the vegetable garden every three years. Large interplantings with marigolds will kill nematodes. Professional soil fumigation may be needed.
Holes appear in leaves, stalks or stems of beans, beets, celery, peppers and potatoes and at the bottom of corn ears, breaking the stems.	European corn borer, a 1-inch spotted caterpillar that moves through the stem; stems must be cut to see the borer.	Borers can be removed by hand. Spray plants with a pesticide recommended for vegetables. Remove all infested plants from the garden in fall.

PROBLEM	CAUSE	SOLUTION
Plants do not develop; full-grown plants may wilt and die. Root crops, especially onions, have tunnels and rot.	Maggots—legless, wormlike, white or yellow pests ⅓ inch long that enter the plant through the roots.	Wood ashes around plant bases deter maggots. Or use an insecticide recommended for vegetables in the soil. Do not fertilize with manure, which attracts maggot-breeding flies.
Colorless areas appear on the leaf surfaces of peppers, tomatoes, cucumbers, eggplant and squash.	Leaf miners, which are tiny maggots.	Cut off and destroy infested leaves. Keep the area well weeded. Treat with a pesticide recommended for vegetables. Remove and destroy infested plants in fall.
Plants, especially tomatoes, weaken and become discolored. When plants are shaken, a large cloud of white insects appears.	Whitefly, a tiny, ¹⁄₁₆-inch insect that sucks on plant leaves.	Treat plants with an insecticidal soap. Flypaper may attract and kill whiteflies. Do not buy plants that show signs of whitefly.
Foliage of beans, lettuce, potatoes, squash and tomatoes starts to yellow, beginning at the edges; leaves begin to curl up. Plants may be stunted.	Leafhoppers, light green or gray winged insects up to ⅕ inch long.	Heavy sprays of water can knock the insects off plants. Or use an insecticide recommended for vegetables.
Vines of squash, pumpkins and cucumbers suddenly wilt; little piles of a yellowish substance appear on stems.	Squash vine borer, a 1-inch white caterpillar with a brown head. Stems must be cut to see the borer.	Hand-pick borers. Cut out damaged stems and pile soil over the tips to foster new growth. Destroy vines after harvest.
Leaves of beans, cucumbers, eggplant or tomatoes have yellow blotches and are mottled with black specks on the undersides. Later, webs form on plants.	Spider mites, almost microscopic pests. The black specks are the mites.	As mites thrive in hot, dry weather, keep plants well watered and mist the undersides of the foliage. Spray with an insecticidal soap or a miticide recommended for vegetables.
Small, round holes with brown edges appear in artichoke buds, stems and foliage.	Artichoke plume moth. The moth lays eggs on the plant and the larva bores into the artichoke.	Destroy infested plants. Apply an insecticide safe for vegetables; do so repeatedly until all signs of the moth and larva disappear.
Foliage and fruit of tomatoes, potatoes, eggplant and peppers are devoured.	Tomato hornworm, a 4-inch green worm with white bands and horns.	Hand-pick. Treat plants with *Bacillus thuringiensis,* called Bt.
Leaves develop white, yellow or brown blotches, distortion or curling, then wither, turn brown and die. Any vegetable, but primarily onions, may be affected.	Thrips, slender insects just barely visible to the eye.	Treat with an insecticide recommended for vegetables when damage first occurs. If the problem persists, remove infested plants. Aluminum foil mulch is a deterrent.

TIPS AND TECHNIQUES

THE EDIBLE LANDSCAPE

When you want to fill your garden with colorful, attractive plants and still be able to enjoy the taste of fresh, home-grown produce, the solution is to create an edible landscape. A number of vegetables that have appealing foliage, flowers and fruit can be planted in flower beds. For example, eggplant grows in a shrubby form and has pink flowers *(right, center)* before it develops into shiny purple or white fruit. Rhubarb and Swiss chard have rich green leaves on bright red-purple stalks. Asparagus plants produce tall, delicate, fernlike foliage. Hot pepper plants have glossy foliage and shiny, brightly colored fruit. Varieties of lettuce that have rich green, wavy leaves tinged with red can be used to trim a flower bed *(right, bottom)*. The low-growing, lacy foliage of carrots and parsnips forms an attractive border. Scarlet runner beans *(right, top),* snap beans and vining cucumbers can be used as screens against a fence or a trellis.

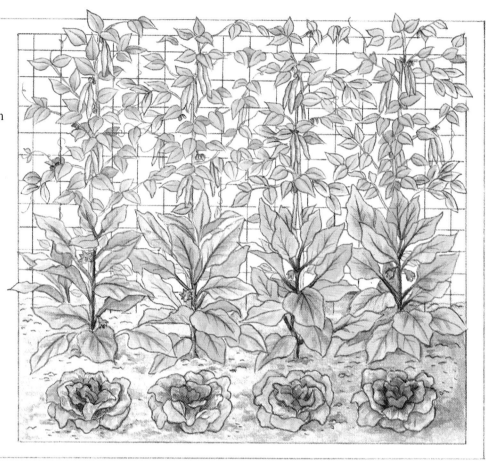

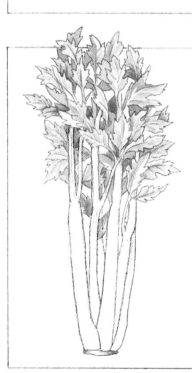

BLANCHING FOR A GOURMET TREAT

Some gardeners—and gourmets—are avid fans of blanched vegetables —those that are pale, almost white, instead of green. Blanching is achieved by mounding soil over the vegetables as they grow so that no light can reach them. Opponents say that blanching lessens vitamin content, but advocates of the technique believe that blanching makes the vegetable more tender and gives it a mild, subtle flavor. The most common candidates for blanching are the vegetables that produce edible stalks or spears, such as celery and asparagus.

CROPS TO IMPROVE THE SOIL

After the garden is harvested in autumn, planting a cover crop, also called green manure, will prevent erosion, add nutrients to the soil, improve drainage and choke out weeds. Green manure is a crop grown not for its edible or ornamental value, but for its benefits to the soil.

If you have a large vegetable garden and will not be growing crops on the entire space during the summer, plant a cover crop instead of allowing the land to stand fallow. Move the cover crop from one area to another each year for a regular program of soil improvement.

Annual ryegrass is a popular cover crop that grows during the fall and can be tilled under just before spring planting so the soil is at its best for the growing season. Legumes are good summer cover crops because they add nitrogen to the soil.

SOAKING SEEDS FOR A FAST START

Most summer vegetables germinate quickly, within 10 days, but a few, such as carrots, celery, okra and parsnips, have seeds that can take as long as three weeks to germinate. These seeds can be speeded along by soaking them in warm water —approximately 100° F—for 24 hours prior to sowing. The soaking also causes a slight increase in the percentage of seeds that will germinate.

Tiny seeds that are difficult to handle, such as celeriac and celery seeds, may be placed in a fine-mesh strainer or in a cheescloth bag for soaking. After soaking, the seeds should not be allowed to dry out, but should be sown immediately, while they are still damp.

Bean seeds, which are extremely susceptible to rot and fungus, should never be soaked before sowing.

GARDENING WITH CHILDREN

If you teach children to garden, they will experience a joy that will be with them the rest of their lives. To encourage children to garden, it is important to have them grow vegetables that will mature quickly so that they can see the results of their efforts right away.

Large vegetable seeds are the easiest for children to handle; corn, beans, beets, carrots and seed potatoes are all good choices. Children also enjoy raising colorful tomato plants. There are varieties of both full-sized beefsteak and cherry tomatoes that mature quickly; see pages 130 and 131.

MAKING THE MOST OF SMALL SPACES

When garden space is limited, the right combination of compact plants and a variety of containers can be used to produce vegetables. Anything from clay pots to wooden barrels, plastic buckets and discarded tires will hold your crops. Patios, balconies and porches can be transformed into vegetable gardens.

Hot peppers *(above)* and eggplant are compact plants that are suitable for container growing. Full-sized tomatoes and cucumbers are available on compact plants. Root crops such as beets and carrots take up little space, and some vegetables—garlic, leeks and onions —don't mind being crowded.

Summer annuals may be mixed with vegetables in containers to add a colorful finishing touch to your garden.

NATURAL INSECT REPELLENT

Certain plants will help to keep unwanted insects out of your vegetable garden. Garlic *(above, behind lettuce)* repels aphids. Radishes can be planted near beans, cucumbers, eggplants, squash and tomatoes to discourage beetles and mites.

Nasturtiums keep aphids, beetles and squash bugs away. Plant beans near potatoes to repel Mexican bean beetles. Marigolds can be fatal to nematodes and will deter Colorado potato beetles. Locate tomato plants near asparagus to discourage asparagus beetles.

6
DICTIONARY OF SUMMER VEGETABLES

The word "vegetable" embraces an array of roots, stems, fruits, buds, leaves and flowers with tastes, textures, shapes and colors diverse enough to satisfy the most eclectic of palates. Summer vegetables are those that share the need for warm summer weather if they are to germinate and flourish. The dictionary that follows describes more than 40 kinds of summer vegetables, each with its unique needs and characteristics. They are arranged alphabetically by their common names; their Latin, or botanical, names follow. Some entries are accompanied by multiple photographs to show differences in shape and color.

Each entry specifies the conditions a plant needs for optimum growth and when a technique such as staking is called for. When to plant and harvest are described, along with the approximate number of days each variety needs to mature. Actual days to harvest will depend on climate, soil condition and the gardener's preference. A zucchini, for instance, may be recommended for harvest in 48 days, when it should be about 8 inches long and at its best in flavor and texture. But the gardener may choose to let the zucchini grow another few weeks into a 2-foot-long showpiece.

Most vegetables have several varieties with varying traits. Some come in both standard and hybrid varieties. Standard varieties are those that have not been crossed artificially. Hybrids, which are crosses between parents with different traits, have been bred for higher yield, better flavor and greater resistance to disease. Different varieties have different degrees of sturdiness; plants described as tolerant of a disease or pest will do better than ordinary plants but not as well as those described as resistant.

Vegetables are generally planted anew each year, since most of them are annuals—plants that live their life cycle in a single growing season. Some vegetables, like beets, are biennials; they develop roots and foliage one year, and produce flowers and fruit the next. They are, however, ordinarily harvested at the end of their first growing season, when their edible roots are at their best. A few vegetables, such as asparagus and rhubarb, are perennials; once planted, they continue producing crops for years.

'GREEN GLOBE' ARTICHOKE

Acorn Squash
see Winter Squash

—

Artichoke
Cynara scolymus

Artichokes are large, succulent flower buds with thick, heavy scales. The buds are the edible parts of the plant and are harvested before they open. Some gardeners leave a bud or two on the plant for their ornamental value; the buds open into broad, bright purple, thistle-like flowers. The plant grows to 4 feet wide and 4 feet tall with silvery green, fernlike foliage. Artichokes are perennial plants in mild-winter areas where temperatures do not drop below 20° F and damage or kill them. In cold-winter areas that have a long growing season, artichokes must be planted year after year.

Selected varieties
'Green Globe,' 100 days from seed to ripe fruit. The standard artichoke variety. The plant produces large, round buds with solid centers and green bracts (petal-like leaves that surround the heart), which sometimes have a purple base.

Growing conditions
Artichokes may be started from seeds or from root divisions. Seeds can be started outdoors in spring after all danger of frost has passed; germination requires 12 to 15 days. Sow the seeds ½ inch deep and 1 to 2 feet apart. When the seedlings are several inches tall, thin them to about 4 feet apart. In cold areas that have a short growing season, the seeds should be started indoors six to eight weeks before the last frost date, then transplanted into the garden.

Seedlings started indoors and root divisions can be planted in the garden after all danger of frost has passed. Plant them 6 inches deep and about 4 feet apart.

Artichokes do best in regions with long, cool summers, such as the California coast. They require rich, well-drained soil. They will not grow where their roots are waterlogged. When growing artichokes as perennials in areas with cool winter temperatures, apply mulch to protect the plants.

Fertilize perennial artichokes in fall after the last harvest or in spring when growth starts. Feed artichokes grown as annuals when they are first planted and again when they are 24 inches high.

Artichokes grown as perennials need to be divided every three to four years or they will cease to produce. This can be done by cutting the roots of old artichoke plants into several sections and planting the new divisions.

Artichokes are susceptible to damage from aphids, slugs, snails and the artichoke plume moth.

Harvesting
Artichokes should be harvested when the flower buds are still closed and about 4 inches across. With a sharp knife, cut the stem 1 to 2 inches below the base of the bud. To encourage further growth, cut the stalks of perennial artichokes to the ground after harvest.

—

Asparagus
Asparagus officinalis

Asparagus is a perennial vegetable that takes three years to start producing edible spears and then continues producing for 12 or more years. From the first spring, spear tips will push through the soil, but the gardener must be patient. If the plant is to develop a strong root system, the first spears must be left unharvested. From them will develop lateral branches and sprawling fernlike foliage up to 3 feet tall. In the third year, when new spears emerge and grow to about 7 inches high, they can be harvested.

Selected varieties

'*California 500*,' three years from seed to harvest. An early variety, tender and never stringy. This commercial hybrid, bred for farmers in warm regions, is also available to the home gardener. Can produce without winter frost but does not thrive in areas of extreme heat. Resistant to asparagus rust.

'*Mary Washington*,' three years. The variety most widely available to the home gardener. Thick, heavy, straight green stalks tinged with purple. Resistant to asparagus rust. '*UC 157*,' three years. Produces from three to five spears in a cluster rather than the open, random pattern of other varieties. The spears are deep green, smooth and cylindrical. Resistant to fusarium root rot.

'*Waltham Washington*,' three years. This is an improved hybrid descendant of '*Mary Washington*' with increased resistance to asparagus rust.

Growing conditions

Most varieties of asparagus must be grown where winter temperatures fall below 20° F. Without freezing soil the plants will not produce. The exception is the variety '*California 500*,' which has been bred to produce in warm regions.

Asparagus can be grown from seeds or from purchased roots. Neither type can be harvested before the third year, but plants started from roots will produce more spears in that year than plants started from seeds. Seeds should be started indoors in winter or outdoors after the soil has warmed to the 70s. Germination takes from two to three weeks. Seeds started indoors should be set into the soil 3 to 5 inches apart. The second year, plants should be thinned or transplanted to 15 inches apart.

Purchased roots are designated as either one- or two-year plants. The designation refers to the age of the roots; either type must grow in the garden for two years before harvesting is possible. Healthy roots have a spread of about 15 inches; they should be firm and turgid. Plant the roots in late spring, 15 inches apart.

Soil for asparagus should be rich in organic matter and well drained. Add fertilizer to the soil before planting. In subsequent years, fertilize in spring, as growth starts, and in fall, after harvesting. Water regularly, especially when the foliage is developing.

Because asparagus foliage is dense, weeding is difficult. Since asparagus does not compete well with weeds, mulch should be used to keep beds weed-free.

Pests and diseases that can affect asparagus are the asparagus beetle, thrips, rust and fusarium root rot.

Harvesting

Snap spears off with your fingers or cut them with a knife at or just below the soil line. Spears should be cut when they are 6 to 8 inches long, but do not harvest until the plants' third year in the garden. During the first two years, allow the spears to develop into foliage. During the third year, harvest only those spears that are at least 7 inches long and ½ inch thick. Harvest for a period of four weeks. After that, allow new spears to grow into foliage, which will strengthen the plant. In the fourth and later years, harvest for a period of six weeks, leaving later spears to produce foliage.

—

Beans

Beans are a main staple of kitchens all over the world. They come in a broad range of shapes, sizes and colors and have a variety of uses. When they are immature, the entire pod is harvested for eating, as with snap beans; when they are mature, they are shelled and only the beans are eaten, as with lima

'MARY WASHINGTON' ASPARAGUS

'GOLDEN' BEET

'RUBY QUEEN' BEET

beans; they can also be allowed to dry on the plant, and the dry beans used in cooking, as with pinto beans. Although each type of bean has characteristics of its own, members of the bean family share certain traits.

Beans are legumes—plants having roots bearing nodules that contain nitrogen-fixing bacteria. Unless you are sowing in spring *(see below)*, make sure you buy bean seeds that have been treated with a bacterial culture called an inoculant, which stimulates chemical action that enables the beans to make use of the nitrogen in the soil; otherwise they will not yield well.

In soil that is cool and damp bean seeds are subject to fungus and rot. If they are started in spring, therefore, they should be treated with a fungicide instead of an inoculant; the fungicide cancels the effect of the inoculant. Whichever you choose, purchase treated seeds from a garden center or a seed catalog; saving seeds from your old plants is not recommended.

All beans are susceptible to damage from certain diseases and insects. To help control these problems, rotate the crops every year, and at the end of the growing season, remove and destroy all dried plant growth.

For specific varieties, see Dry Beans; Garbanzo Beans; Horticultural Beans; Lima Beans; Snap Beans; Southern Peas; Soybeans.

Beet

Beta vulgaris, Crassa Group

Beets are sweet-tasting, globular or tapering roots in shades of deep red or purple; a few varieties have gold roots and some have white roots. The flesh of some varieties is marked with concentric circles called zones. The tops are reddish green and leafy and grow to about 18 inches; they can be cooked and eaten as greens. Beets can be left in the soil for two years, but roots produced the second year are usually less tender and less tasty than those of the first year.

Selected varieties

'Detroit Dark Red,' 60 days from seed to ripe fruit. Round, with deep red skin; flesh is bright red, smooth and zoneless. Finely grained, rich and very sweet. Best harvested when small. *'Golden,'* 55 days. Fast-growing. Its golden roots do not bleed during cooking. Retains its tender texture even when allowed to grow large. Sow seeds heavily; germination is not high.

'Lutz Green Leaf,' 80 days. Also called *'Winter Keeper'* because it stores well. Tapered, with purplish red skin; flesh is dark red and zoned. Retains its sweetness even if allowed to grow to a large size. *'Red Ace,'* 53 days. This globe-shaped hybrid has increased vigor, with very dark red, smooth, zoneless flesh.

'Red Ball,' 60 days. Globe-shaped, with deep red skin; flesh is dark red, smooth and zoneless. Best variety for areas with cold spring weather. *'Ruby Queen,'* 52 days. Early variety. Globe-shaped, solid red, with short, dark green leaves that redden over time.

Growing Conditions

Beets are started from seeds. In early spring, as soon as the soil can be worked, the seeds should be sown in their permanent location. Like other root crops, they cannot be transplanted; a move would cause root deformity.

Sow seeds ½ inch deep and 1 inch apart. As a beet seed is actually a fruit containing two or three seeds, thinning will need to be done soon after germination, which takes 10 to 14 days, or overcrowding will occur. Seedlings should be thinned to 3 to 4 inches apart. The thinnings may be used in soups and stews.

Beets are tolerant of heat and resistant to light frosts, so they have a long growing season. For a continuous supply of beets, sow seeds every three weeks from early spring until two months before the first fall frost date.

The best flavor is obtained when beets mature quickly, which requires a rich, loose, well-drained soil. Beets do best in neutral soil; apply lime to acid soil. Add 5-10-5 fertilizer to the soil before sowing. Water regularly to prevent toughness, especially during hot spells.

Beets are relatively insect- and disease-free; the one pest that may damage the plants is the leaf miner.

Harvesting
Pull beets from the ground when they are 2 to 3 inches across; gently move the soil away from the root to check the size. Light frost will not damage beets, but they should be harvested before the ground freezes hard. Leave 1 inch of stem on the beet to prevent bleeding during cooking.

—

Black-eyed Peas
see Southern Peas

—

Carrot
Daucus carota sativis

Carrots are yellow-orange roots that grow beneath bright green, finely cut foliage that can reach 20 inches in height. The roots are generally long, slender and tapered, although some varieties have round, short or wedge-shaped roots. Carrot plants can be left in the garden for two years, but they are usually less tender and less tasty in the second year. Selection of a carrot variety should be based on soil characteristics. The shorter types should be chosen in areas where the soil is heavy; the smaller roots are less likely to be deformed by heavy soil.

Selected varieties
'Danvers Half Long,' 75 days from seed to ripe fruit. Perfectly cylindrical carrot 7 inches long. Deep red-orange skin with bright orange, finely grained flesh. 'Goldinhart,' 70 days. Also known as 'Red Cored Chantenay.' Bright golden carrot 5 inches long and 2½ inches thick. 'Juwarot,' 70 days. Dark orange, tapered carrot up to 8 inches in length. 'Little Finger,' 65 days. This variety is only 3½ inches long and ⅝ inch wide. It is especially tender and is a gourmet treat when cooked whole.

'Nantes Half Long,' 70 days. Slim, cylindrical, 6- to 7-inch orange carrot is smooth and finely grained. 'Short 'n Sweet,' 68 days. Bright orange to the center, 4 inches long and 2 inches thick. Excellent for container growing. 'Tiny Sweet,' 65 days. A 3-inch-long midget carrot.

Growing conditions
Carrots are grown from seeds, which can be sown directly in the garden in spring, as soon as the soil can be worked. Carrot plants cannot be transplanted; a move can cause deformities in the roots.

Sow seeds ½ inch deep. Germination takes two to three weeks. When plants begin to develop, thin them to 3 inches apart. The thinnings can be used in cooking. To have a continuous supply of carrots, sow seeds in succession every three weeks until two months before the first fall frost is expected.

Carrots do best in temperatures between 40° and 80° F. They should not be grown during the summer in areas of extreme heat.

Good soil is critical for growing carrots; unless it is light and loose, carrots will not form properly. Incorporate large amounts of organic matter and add 5-10-10 fertilizer to the soil before sowing. Keep the soil evenly moist to prevent the carrots from splitting.

Carrot plants can be damaged by damping-off, aster yellows, root maggots and leafhoppers.

'JUWAROT' CARROT

'SHORT 'N SWEET' CARROT

'ALABASTER' CELERIAC

'UTAH 52-70R IMPROVED' CELERY

Harvesting

Carrots should be harvested when they are 2 inches or less in diameter; gently move the soil away from the root to check its size. Smaller carrots generally have better flavor. Although carrots will not be harmed by light frost, they should be harvested before the ground freezes hard.

Celeriac

Apium graveolens rapaceum

Celeriac is a 4-inch, globular, rough and knobby root that has a flavor similar to celery but stronger and a little nuttier. The plant grows to 2 feet tall, with foliage almost identical to that of celery. It is closely related to celery and is sometimes called root celery or turnip celery, but unlike celery, it is always eaten cooked, never raw.

Selected varieties

'Alabaster,' 120 days from seed to ripe fruit. Stores well over winter.

Growing conditions

The cultivation of celeriac is very similar to that of celery. Celeriac can be started from seeds. Because of its long growing season, seeds should be started indoors about 10 weeks before transplanting into the garden. Germination takes 21 days.

When night temperatures cease to drop below 55° F, celeriac can be planted outside. Space the plants 6 to 12 inches apart. Set the root at soil level. If side shoots from the main root develop, they should be removed.

Soil for celeriac should be rich in organic matter, water-retentive and extremely fertile. Fertilize the soil with 5-10-5 prior to planting and again once every month. Water regularly. Add mulch to keep the soil cool and moist.

Celeriac plants are generally insect- and disease-free.

Harvesting

Celeriac can be harvested any time after it has grown to a height of 2 inches or more. Lift the whole plant from the ground and discard the top. When frost threatens, place mulch over the tops of the plants to extend the season for several weeks.

Celery

Apium graveolens dulce

Celery is a leafy, bushy plant that grows to 30 inches tall and produces edible, elongated, light green or yellow leaf stalks usually from 6 to 9 inches long. The stalks are crisp, crunchy and high in fiber, and can be eaten raw or cooked. Celery is a biennial, but it is grown as an annual.

Selected varieties.

'Fordhook,' 130 days from seed to ripe fruit. Stocky and compact plant between 15 and 18 inches in height. Stalks are crisp and juicy with a full heart. Stores well.

'Giant Pascal,' 125 days. A plant approximately 24 inches high produces a thick, solid stalk 8 inches long that has a cream-colored heart. The foliage is dark green. Stores well.

'Golden Detroit,' 115 days. Dwarf plant with yellow stalks.

'Golden Self-Blanching,' 115 days. A plant 20 inches tall. Stalks are thick-ribbed and clear waxen yellow in color. The stalks and heart are stringless, and have a nutty flavor. The plant does well in areas with cold spring temperatures. Blight tolerant.

'Utah 52-70R Improved,' 105 days. Grows 26 inches high and has crisp, thick, dark green stalks 12 inches long. Resistant to brown check, Western celery mosaic and black heart.

Growing conditions

Celery needs a growing season of

approximately four months of 70° F weather; it is therefore a good summer crop for the northern United States. It does not thrive in areas with hot, dry summers.

Celery is grown from seeds, which may be started indoors 10 to 12 weeks before being transplanted into the garden. Germination takes 21 to 25 days. Alternatively, you may buy seedlings from a garden center. In either case, when seedlings are 3 to 4 inches tall, plant them outdoors 9 to 12 inches apart.

Celery needs soil that is moist, rich in organic matter and has a pH of 6.0 to 7.0. Celery is also a heavy feeder; it requires twice the amount of fertilizer that most vegetables do. Fertilize with 5-10-5 prior to planting and once a month thereafter.

Celery plants can be affected by late blight, black heart, mosaic, brown check, aphids, nematodes and plant bugs.

Harvesting
Celery can be harvested by lifting the entire plant from the ground or by cutting the stalks off at the soil line; or outer stalks can be pulled off without damage to the plant, which will remain intact and continue to grow. Do not let celery continue growing past its maturity date or it will become pithy and hollow.

—

Chick-peas see Garbanzo Beans

—

Chicory
Cichorium intybus

Chicory is a cousin of endive and escarole. Its basal foliage is oblong and grows to 18 inches in a head of large, loosely wrapped, dark green leaves. The leaves are used as salad greens; the roots of 'Magdeburg' chicory are ground and used as a component of or substitute for coffee. Chicory can be grown as a perennial in areas where winter temperatures drop to −20° F. It is generally grown as an annual because if it is left in the ground for more than a season, its roots become invasive.

Selected varieties
'Magdeburg,' 100 days from seed to mature plant. Grown primarily for its roots, which can be roasted for coffee. Foliage resembles that of a dandelion. 'Sugarhat,' 86 days. Grown for tender, sweet yet tangy leaves that are long and oval, resembling romaine lettuce.

'Witloof,' 110 days. Sometimes called French endive or Belgian endive. The light green tops are tall and leafy. This variety is grown primarily for its roots. The roots are harvested in fall, then replanted indoors or in a cold frame, where they produce small clusters of leaves called chicons. These chicons, slender, elongated heads that come to a point, are very sweet and tender.

Growing conditions
Chicory is grown from seeds planted directly in the soil about the time of the last spring frost. In the hot South and West, it can be sown in late summer for a winter crop. Seeds should be planted ½ inch deep and 4 inches apart. After germination, which takes seven to 10 days, plants should be thinned to 12 inches apart.

Chicory grown for its roots (either 'Magdeburg' or 'Witloof') must not be allowed to go to seed in the fall; the roots become bitter. Therefore, do not sow chicory seed for coffee or chicons more than three and a half months before the first fall frost.

Soil for chicory should have a neutral pH. When plants are grown for foliage, average soil is adequate. When plants are grown for roots, soil must be rich in organic matter and constantly moist.

Fertilize prior to planting and again after two months. A fertilizer

'SUGARHAT' CHICORY

'EARLY SUNGLOW' YELLOW CORN

'HOW SWEET IT IS' WHITE CORN

low in nitrogen, such as 5-10-10, should be used when growing plants for roots; 5-10-5 should be used for foliage crops.

Chicory is free of insects and diseases.

Harvesting

Chicory foliage can be harvested as often as needed up until just before the first frost, when the leaves begin to acquire a bitter taste. If the roots are left in the ground all winter, they will produce new leaves for harvest in spring. After the leaves have been harvested, the plant will produce a tall stem with light blue flowers.

Chicory grown for its roots is harvested in fall after the first light frost but before the ground freezes hard. When 'Magdeburg' chicory is intended for coffee, it should be used right after harvest.

—

Corn

Zea mays rugosa

Corn is a grassy plant that grows up to 9 feet tall and usually produces one or two ears with yellow, white or bicolored kernels. The kernels are square, and varieties with larger kernels have fewer rows of kernels per cob.

Corn is sweetest and most flavorful when it is cooked within minutes of picking, which is why home gardeners give so much space to this space-taking vegetable.

Beginning in the early 1970s, seed breeders developed varieties of "supersweet" corn. These varieties—also called "shrunken" for the appearance of their seeds —remain sweet for a longer period of time (10 to 14 days) after harvest because their sugar content is slow to convert to starch. The home gardener who cooks corn as soon as it is harvested does not need to grow one of the supersweet corns. These varieties are meant for corn that will be stored before cooking.

Popcorn (Zea mays praecox) resembles sweet corn, except that the kernels are pointed and explode when subjected to heat.

Yellow varieties

'Earliking,' 66 days from seed to ripe fruit. A plant that may yield three ears per stalk. Grows to 5 feet tall. Good for short northern seasons. Cobs are 7½ inches long, with 10 to 12 rows of kernels. Hybrid. 'Early Golden Giant,' 63 days. Husky, 5-foot stalks produce 8-inch ears of corn with 14 to 18 rows of kernels.

'Early Sunglow,' 63 days. Four-foot plant that produces 6- to 7-inch ears with 12 rows of very sweet kernels. A good variety for areas with cool spring weather, since seeds can survive in cold soil. Hybrid. 'Early Xtra Sweet,' 70 days. A supersweet hybrid, 5 to 6 feet tall. Ears are 7 to 9 inches long with 12 to 16 rows of kernels. Sweeter than standard varieties, matures early.

'Golden Beauty,' 73 days. Hybrid variety to 5½ feet tall, with 7-inch cobs, 12 to 14 rows of kernels. 'Golden Cross Bantam,' 85 days. Seed companies consider this variety, developed in the early 1900s, the standard for rating the quality of other yellow varieties. Plants are 6 to 7 feet tall, producing 8-inch ears with 10 to 14 rows of large, light yellow kernels. Hybrid.

'Golden Jubilee,' 84 days. Ears are 9 inches long with 16 to 18 rows of kernels. Hybrid. 'Golden Midget,' 60 days. A novelty. Plants 30 inches high produce 4-inch ears with 8 rows of kernels. 'Illini Xtra Sweet,' 83 days. A supersweet hybrid variety with twice the sugar content of standard corn. Stores well. Plants are 6½ feet tall. Ears are 8 inches long, with 14 to 18 rows of kernels.

'Iochief,' 83 days. This hybrid is more drought-tolerant and wind-resistant than most corns. Ears are 9 to 10 inches long with 14 to 18 rows of kernels on 6½-foot plants. '*Jubilee*,' 81 days. A long-lasting variety good for freezing or canning. Does well in cool areas. The plant is 7½ feet tall with ears 7 to 9 inches long. Hybrid.

'*Kandy Korn*,' 85 days. This hybrid has a high sugar content and a high rate of germination. Does well in cool areas. Husks and stalks are tinged in burgundy. Plants are 8 to 9 feet tall and produce 8-inch ears with 14 to 16 rows of kernels. '*Polar Vee*,' 53 days. One of the earliest hybrids, good for areas with a short growing season and a cold climate. Ears are 4 to 6 inches long with 12 rows of kernels.

'*Seneca Chief*,' 82 days. Plants are 6 feet tall; cobs are slender, 8½ inches long and have 12 rows of kernels.

'*Stylepak*,' 86 days. Good variety for freezing and canning. Thick, 8-inch ears with 18 to 20 rows of kernels. Tolerant of smut and wilt.

'*Super Sweet*,' 89 days. A supersweet hybrid with 7½- to 8-inch ears and 16 to 18 rows of kernels. Plants are 6½ feet high. Kernels are more tender than other supersweet varieties because the husks are thicker and provide more protection against the elements.

White varieties

'*How Sweet It Is*,' 80 days from seed to ripe fruit. This supersweet hybrid keeps well. Plants grow to 7 feet. Cobs are 8 inches long, with 16 to 18 rows of kernels. '*Silver Queen*,' 92 days. Seed companies consider this hybrid the standard for rating other varieties of white corn. Ears are 8 to 9 inches long with 14 to 16 rows of very tender and sweet kernels. Plant is 7 to 8 feet tall. Does not survive in cool soil in spring. Resistant to wilt.

Bicolored varieties

'*Butter & Sugar*,' 73 days from seed to ripe fruit. This is the original variety of corn with both yellow and white kernels. Ears are 6½ to 8 inches long, with 12 to 14 rows

of kernels on a plant 5 to 6 feet in height. Hybrid.

'*Butterfruit Bicolor*,' 76 days. A supersweet hybrid. Small kernels in 16 to 18 rows on 8-inch ears. Plant grows to 7 feet. Good for freezing and canning. '*Calypso*,' 83 days. Small kernels in 18 to 22 rows on 8½-inch ears. Plant grows to 8 feet tall.

Popping varieties

'*Cream Puff Hybrid*,' 105 days. The plant is 8½ feet tall and a heavy yielder of yellow popcorn. '*Peppy Hybrid*,' 90 days from seed to ripe fruit. A high-yielding 6-foot plant with white kernels on 4-inch ears. The fastest-growing popcorn variety; good for areas with a short growing season.

Growing conditions

Corn is grown from seed. It does not transplant well, and should be sown directly in the soil after all danger of frost has passed and the soil has warmed to 50° F. Seeds should be planted 2 inches deep and 4 to 6 inches apart in rows 2 to 3 feet apart. Once plants are a few inches high, thin them to 12 to 14 inches. Do not grow corn plants too close together; crowding reduces yield.

To guarantee a supply of corn throughout the summer, either plant several varieties of early-, midseason- and late-maturing corn, or plant seeds in succession every two weeks until early summer.

Corn must be planted in a block of the same type and of at least three rows rather than in a straight line; this ensures pollination and development. Yellow hybrid corn must be planted downwind from white corn, or cross-pollination will occur and the white corn will not develop. The supersweet hybrids should be grown in a separate area at least 700 feet away from other varieties to prevent cross-pollination, which will result in tough, tasteless kernels.

Popcorn is grown in the same way as other corn. To prevent

'BUTTERFRUIT BICOLOR' CORN

POPPING CORN

'SWEET SLICE' CUCUMBER

'WHITE WONDER' SLICING CUCUMBER

cross-pollination, plant it at least 100 feet from other varieties.

Some corn seed is treated with a fungicide to prevent rotting before germination. This is necessary where the soil is continuously damp and cold in spring.

Corn does best in areas with long, hot summers. Soil should be rich and neutral. Fertilize with 5-10-5 prior to planting, then when the plants are 8 inches tall and again when they are 18 inches tall. If supersweet hybrids are to germinate, the soil must be warm and twice as moist as would be needed for a regular variety of corn.

Corn is a shallow-rooted plant, so be careful when weeding not to disturb the plants' roots. Mulch can be applied to the soil, or you can follow the Indian custom of interplanting corn with pumpkins or squash; these low-growing vegetables prevent weeds from developing.

Problems that can develop with corn are corn borer, corn earworm, corn maggot, smut and wilt. Wilt is generally a problem only with nonhybrid varieties.

Harvesting
To retain as much sweetness as possible, most varieties of corn should be harvested just before cooking. The cobs are ready to harvest when the silks—the hairlike growths that emerge at the tips of the husks—start to turn brown and damp. To test for readiness, open a husk slightly and prick a kernel with your fingernail. If it bursts with its milk, it is ready to pick.

To harvest, hold the ear near the bottom and break it off the plant with a downward, twisting motion. If there are two ears per plant, the top one will be ready a day or two before the lower one.

Harvest ears of popcorn at the end of the growing season and allow them to dry in a warm indoor area.

—

Cowpeas see Southern Peas

Cress see Watercress

—

Cucumbers
Cucumis sativus

Most cucumbers are cylindrical, dark green fruits; most of them grow on sprawling, vining plants that reach 6 to 8 feet long and have rough, medium green, three-pointed leaves and 1-inch yellow flowers. There are also several varieties that grow on compact, bushy plants; these are ideal for gardens with limited space.

Varieties of cucumbers have been developed specifically for slicing and for pickling. Slicing cucumbers are cylindrical and can grow to 10 inches long. Pickling cucumbers are shorter and more blocky. Some varieties are called "burpless." These cucumbers are supposedly easier to digest than other varieties, although the reason for this has not been determined.

Cucumbers are also classed according to their reproductive traits. Most plants have both male and female flowers. Some have only female flowers; those that do yield more cucumbers and mature earlier than plants that have both male and female flowers. When you buy seeds for female-flowering plants, the packet will contain a pollinator. There are also self-fertilizing varieties, which form fruit without pollination and are truly seedless. These varieties must be isolated to prevent cross-pollination by other varieties. The varieties listed below have both male and female flowers, except where noted.

Slicing varieties
'Armenian,' 70 days from seed to ripe fruit. A ribbed, light green cucumber that grows to 3 feet in length. Harvested at 2½ inches across for best flavor and texture. Nonhybrid. 'Burpee Hybrid II,' 55 days. Fruit is straight and 8½

inches long. Has only female flowers. Resistant to cucumber mosaic virus and downy mildew.

'Burpless Hybrid #26,' 70 days. Fruit is 10 inches long, smooth and narrow. Plant is tolerant of mildew. *'Green Knight,'* 60 days. Thick-skinned fruit that can grow to 18 inches long but is best harvested at 8 inches. Heat-resistant. Burpless. Hybrid.

'Marketmore 76,' 67 days. Straight, 8- to 9-inch fruit. This variety does well in cool northern climates. Long-lasting fruit. Resistant to cucumber mosaic virus and scab. Nonhybrid. *'Salad Bar,'* 57 days. Slightly tapered, 8-inch, dark green fruit. Resistant to several diseases. Hybrid.

'Slicemaster,' 55 days. Up to 8 inches long. Has only female flowers. Tolerant of downy and powdery mildew, angular leaf spot, anthracnose, scab and cucumber mosaic virus. Hybrid. *'Straight Eight,'* 63 days. Lightly striped, straight fruit 8 inches in length. Nonhybrid.

'Super Slice,' 64 days. Slim fruit 9 inches long. Resistant to scab and tolerant of cucumber mosaic virus. Hybrid. *'Sweet Slice,'* 62 days. Tender-skinned 12-inch fruit with white flesh. Tolerant of downy and powdery mildew, leaf spot, cucumber mosaic virus, anthracnose and scab. Burpless. Hybrid.

'Sweet Success,' 58 days. The first truly seedless cucumber, with thin skin and sweet, crispy flesh. Grows to 14 inches long. Burpless. Self-fertilizing. Resistant to cucumber mosaic virus, scab and leaf spot. Hybrid. *'Victory,'* 62 days. Slim, smooth, firm and straight fruit to 8 inches long. Has only female flowers. Tolerant of cucumber mosaic virus, downy mildew, powdery mildew and scab; resistant to leaf spot and anthracnose. Hybrid.

'White Wonder,' 60 days. A novelty; the cucumber has snow white skin. Grows 8 to 10 inches long; meat is firm and crisp. Nonhybrid.

'Whopper Improved,' 55 days. Thick 10-inch fruit. Almost seedless. Has only female flowers. Tolerant of powdery mildew and downy mildew; resistant to scab, cucumber mosaic virus, leaf spot and anthracnose. Hybrid.

Pickling varieties

'Cherokee,' 55 days from seed to ripe fruit. Skin is smooth and deep green. Plant is resistant to powdery mildew and downy mildew, anthracnose and angular leaf spot. Hybrid. *'Earlipick,'* 53 days. A blocky, 5-inch-long cucumber. The plant has only female flowers. Tolerant of powdery mildew and cucumber mosaic virus; resistant to scab. Hybrid.

'Liberty,' 54 days. Blocky fruit 3½ inches long. Has female flowers only. Tolerant of powdery mildew, downy mildew and leaf spot; resistant to scab and cucumber mosaic virus. Hybrid. *'Luckystrike,'* 52 days. Compact plant with medium-sized fruit. Good in cool-weather areas. Has only female flowers. Tolerant of most diseases. Hybrid.

'Saladin,' 55 days. Bright green, 5-inch fruit has only female flowers. Tolerant of powdery mildew and bacterial wilt; resistant to cucumber mosaic virus. Hybrid.

Bush varieties

'Bush Crop,' 60 days from seed to ripe fruit. Slicing. A compact, bushy plant with short vines and cucumbers 7 inches long. Hybrid. *'Bush Pickle,'* 48 days. Pickling. Straight, 4- to 5-inch fruit produced on plants 3 feet tall and wide. Nonhybrid.

'Patio Pik,' 50 days. Pickling. Excellent for growing in tubs and baskets. Has only female flowers. Tolerant of several diseases. Hybrid. *'Pot Luck,'* 55 days. Slicing. Good for the small garden and for container growing. Grows to 18 inches with fruit 7 inches long. Tolerant of cucumber mosaic virus and scab. Hybrid.

'SALADIN' PICKLING CUCUMBER

'BUSH CROP' CUCUMBER

103

'GREAT NORTHERN' DRY BEAN

Growing conditions

Cucumbers are started from seeds planted directly in the soil in spring, after all danger of frost has passed. Seeds should be sown 1 inch deep and 4 to 6 inches apart. Germination takes about seven days. When seedlings are 2 inches tall, thin them to 12 inches apart.

When varieties having all female flowers are used, be sure to mark the male pollinator so that it is not accidentally thinned out. Male plants have green seeds; female plants have beige seeds. Use one male plant for every five or six females. The male flowers will blossom first. The fruit will not form until after the female flowers have bloomed.

Where the growing season is five months or more, a second sowing in midseason is suggested for a second crop.

Cucumber vines can be left to grow along the ground or they can be trained on a trellis, pole, fence or other support.

Cucumbers do best in warm, mild climates. The soil must be rich in organic matter, light, moist and well drained. Fertilize the soil before planting and then monthly with 5-10-5.

Cucumbers are susceptible to damage from a number of diseases and insects. These include cucumber mosaic virus, downy mildew, powdery mildew, scab, bacterial wilt, angular leaf spot, anthracnose, striped cucumber beetles, aphids and mites.

Harvesting

Pickling cucumbers are usually harvested when small, 1½ to 3 inches long, but they can be allowed to grow longer for large dill pickles. Slicing cucumbers are harvested when they are about 7 inches long. Cut the cucumber from the vine with a knife rather than breaking it off. Cucumbers should be harvested regularly to keep the plant productive.

Dry Beans
Phaseolus vulgaris

Dry beans are certain varieties of the snap bean family (see Snap Beans) that are left on the vine until dried by the sun. When the pods of these varieties mature, they split and the dry beans fall out. Plants grow to about 20 inches tall. The beans are from ¼ to ¾ inch long and are white, yellow, pink, brown, black or speckled, with somewhat variable flavor and many uses in cooking.

Selected varieties
'Black Turtle,' 104 days from seed to dry bean. Tall plants with small black beans in slender pods. This is the variety used in black bean soup. 'Great Northern,' 90 days. Also called navy beans. Pods 3 to 4 inches long filled with large white beans that retain a firm consistency when cooked.

'Pinto,' 85 days. Plants may develop short runners and may be trained on a pole. Pods are 5 inches long and produce deep pink, speckled beans. 'Red Kidney,' 95 days. Large, reddish, flat, kidney-shaped beans in 6-inch pods.

'White Marrowfat,' 100 days. Also called navy beans. Flat, straight pods with five or six large white beans.

Growing conditions
Dry beans mature and produce over a short period of time; to have a continuous supply of beans, make successive plantings every two to three weeks.

After all danger of frost has passed, sow seeds directly in the soil—1 inch deep in heavy soils, 1½ inches deep in sandy soils. Germination takes six days. Seedlings should be thinned to about 5 inches apart, except for the flat-podded varieties, which take slightly more space.

Dry beans do best in areas where summers are warm. The beans will grow in any average, well-drained garden soil with a pH higher than 6.0. Fertilize prior to planting with 5-10-10; no further feeding is needed.

Harvesting
Dry beans can be harvested by pulling pods off the plant just as they begin to split open, or by holding the plant at the base and shaking the beans off into a cheesecloth or a bag. Or the entire plant may be lifted from the soil.

—

Eggplant
Solanum melongena

Eggplant is so named because its fruit was originally small, whitish and egg-shaped. Although some varieties retain this shape, the modern eggplant may be round or elongated and generally has shiny dark purple fruit. The plant is bushy, grows 2 to 3 feet tall, has fuzzy leaves and produces attractive pink flowers that develop into the fruit. Each plant usually produces four or five fruits. There are also varieties called Oriental eggplants, which produce a more slender fruit with a dull skin. The calyx (the end of the stem that looks like a cap on the eggplant) on Oriental eggplant is purple; the calyx of the others is green.

Selected varieties
'Black Beauty,' 80 days from transplanted seedlings to ripe fruit. One of the few nonhybrids grown. Plant is 24 inches tall. Fruit is dark purple, broad and round with a blunt end. 'Beauty Hybrid,' 69 days. Glossy black skin covers firm flesh and rounded fruit. Resistant to fusarium and tobacco mosaic virus.

'Burpee Hybrid,' 70 days. This tall, semispreading plant has oval, medium-sized, glossy, dark purple fruit. 'Dusky Hybrid,' 62 days. The best for areas where the growing season is short. Fruit is firm, slender, oval, medium-sized and jet

black. Plant is highly productive and resistant to tobacco mosaic.

'Easter Egg,' 52 days. Shiny white, egg-shaped fruit that is very ornamental. Resistant to tobacco mosaic virus. 'Ichiban Improved,' 54 days. An Oriental-type hybrid with 8-inch, narrow, cylindrical fruit that has purplish black skin.

'Satin Beauty,' 65 days. An improved, early-maturing hybrid descendant of 'Black Beauty' with deep purplish black fruit. Plant is compact and good for container growing. 'Tycoon,' 54 days. A long, high-yielding, slender, purplish black fruit. Oriental type. Hybrid.

Growing conditions
Eggplant must have a long, warm growing season and is ideal for the Deep South and hot West. It is grown from seeds generally started indoors, eight weeks before the last frost and when night temperatures will not drop below 55° F. Sow seeds ¼ inch deep. Seeds germinate in 10 to 15 days. The seedlings should be planted in the garden 18 to 24 inches apart once the weather has settled and the soil has warmed.

Eggplant may also be grown in containers.

Soil for eggplants should be slightly acid, well drained and rich in organic matter. Fertilize lightly with 5-10-5 at planting time and again when the plants bloom.

Eggplant is susceptible to damage from verticillium wilt, cutworm, flea beetle and Colorado potato beetle. To keep disease to a minimum, do not plant eggplant where tomatoes, peppers or strawberries have been grown in the last three years; all are susceptible to verticillium wilt.

Harvesting
Although an eggplant can grow up to 10 inches in diameter, it is best harvested when 4 to 5 inches across and when the skin is still glossy; when the skin becomes dull the fruit is apt to be bitter.

'BEAUTY HYBRID' EGGPLANT

GARBANZO BEAN

GARLIC

Cut the fruit from the plant with shears, leaving a small piece of stem on the eggplant. Harvesting early will encourage further fruit production within the season.

—

Garbanzo Beans
Cicer arietinium

Garbanzo beans, also called chick-peas, grow on plants that are 12 to 24 inches tall, bushy and somewhat weedy in appearance. Compound leaves are made up of 15 leaflets. Tan-colored beans with a nutty flavor form in short, 1-inch swollen pods. As only one or two wrinkled beans form in each puffy pod and plants are bushy, garbanzo beans require a lot of space for a relatively low yield. The beans are a rich source of starch and protein, and they benefit the soil by replenishing its nitrogen supply.

Selected varieties
There are no named varieties of garbanzo beans; the seeds are sold under the common name. They mature in 100 days from seed to ripe bean.

Growing conditions
Garbanzo beans do best in the hot, dry conditions of the South and West. Start the plants from seeds sown directly in the soil 1 to 1½ inches apart. Germination takes six days. As plants develop, thin them to 6 inches apart.

Garbanzo beans produce and mature over a short period of time; successive plantings ensure a continuous supply.

Soil should be dry and sandy.

Plants are susceptible to mosaic, rust, anthracnose, blight, powdery mildew, aphids, leafhoppers, mites and bean beetles.

Harvesting
Harvest individual pods as they begin to split, or pull the entire plant out of the soil and allow the beans to dry and fall off onto a catch cloth.

Garlic
Allium sativum

Garlic, a pungent member of the onion family, has a bulb made up of seven to 10 cloves encased in a papery white skin. Large flat leaves grow up to 15 inches tall and resemble the leaves of the bearded iris. If allowed to flower, garlic produces globular clusters of attractive, tiny white blooms. Flowering does not affect the quality of the edible cloves. Garlic is a perennial, but in areas of extreme cold it may not survive the winter.

Selected varieties
Although a few varieties of garlic have been developed, they are not widely available to home gardeners. Garlic is usually sold under its common name. The plant matures in 90 days from clove to bulb.

Growing conditions
Garlic is grown not from seed but from individual cloves. You can buy cloves from garden centers or you can use cloves from the supermarket. Break cloves off carefully from the main bulb and plant them directly in the soil 3 to 4 inches apart, pointed side up and deep enough so their tips are just covered.

Garlic is planted in early to middle spring as soon as the ground can be worked for harvest in the fall. In the hot South and West, garlic can be planted in fall for a spring harvest. Cloves will begin to show signs of growth within seven days; the tip of a green stem will emerge from the soil.

Soil for garlic should be well drained, light, sandy and enriched with organic matter. The best growth is obtained when the soil is loose; the pH level can be anywhere in the 5.5 to 8.0 range. Fertilize at planting time and again when the tops are 6 inches tall, using a fertilizer low in nitrogen, such as 5-10-10. Too much nitrogen will cause lush top growth at the expense of the bulbs.

Garlic plants actually repel insects; the plants are also free of disease.

Harvesting

When the foliage starts to turn yellow at the end of the season, bend the tops over at the base without breaking them. This will hasten ripening and drying. Leave the bulbs in the soil for two to three days; then lift them carefully and allow them to dry in the sun. For storage, you can braid the tops *(page 74)* and hang them, or you can keep them in any cool, dark, well-ventilated spot.

After harvesting, save several bulbs for cloves to plant for next year's crop.

—

Green Beans see Snap Beans

—

Horseradish
Armoracia rusticana

The root of the horseradish plant is the source of the hot and zesty grated sauce of the same name. The plant grows to 30 inches tall, has large, coarse leaves and white, seedless flowers. The roots are long, thick and white. Horseradish is a perennial hardy to 10° F, but it is generally grown as an annual, because roots become tough and stringy the second year.

Selected varieties
'Maliner Kren,' 150 days from root cuttings to mature fruit. The standard variety of horseradish, also known as Bohemian horseradish. Straight white roots up to 18 inches in length.

Growing conditions
Horseradish is grown from root cuttings, which may be planted in spring or fall. If you take cuttings from a larger root, cut 6-inch sections as thick as a pencil. Purchased roots have tapered ends; plant

them at an angle, with the slanted end pointing down and the upper end 2 to 3 inches below the soil surface. Space the roots about 1 foot apart. Horseradish does not do well in extreme summer heat.

Soil should be loose, rich and well drained for straight root formation. Horseradish does not do well in sandy soil. Add fertilizer to the soil at planting time.

The flea beetle can cause damage to horseradish plants.

Harvesting
Dig up horseradish roots in autumn and winter as needed; they are best used when fresh. Be sure to remove all roots that will not be used before growth starts the next spring, since remaining roots can become invasive weeds.

—

Horticultural Beans
Phaseolus vulgaris

Horticultural beans, also called field beans or shell beans, are very similar to snap beans, but they are grown for the seeds inside their pods, like peas. It is possible to harvest young beans and eat the pods, but the pods are tough.

Some varieties have colorful pods splashed with crimson or maroon, and some have bicolored beans. The beans range in size from ¼ to ½ inch long, and their texture is mealy and nutty.

Selected varieties
'Dwarf Horticultural,' 65 days from seed to ripe bean. Plants are 18 inches tall; pods are 5 inches long, flat and light green turning red at maturity. *'French Horticultural,'* 68 days. The plant produces short runners but does not need staking. Pods have splashes of red and cream; beans are buff and red. *'White Half Runner,'* 60 days. The plant produces runners 3 feet long but does not need staking. The pods are green and round; seeds

'MALINER KREN' HORSERADISH

'FRENCH HORTICULTURAL' BEAN

JERUSALEM ARTICHOKE

'BROAD LONDON' LEEK

are white. The plant tolerates heat and drought.

Growing conditions

Beans are grown from seeds planted directly in the garden after all danger of frost has passed and the soil is warm. Seeds should be sown 1 inch deep in heavy soils and 1½ inches deep in sandy soils. Germination takes about six days. Seedlings should be thinned to about 5 inches apart.

Beans can be grown in any average, well-drained soil with a pH over 6.0. Before planting, fertilize with 5-10-10; no further feeding is necessary.

Beans are susceptible to damage from anthracnose, blight, powdery mildew, aphids, bean beetles, leafhoppers and mites.

Harvesting

When the beans are mature, either pull the pods off the plant or lift the entire plant from the ground. The beans should be full and plump. Test by harvesting a few as their maturity date approaches; it may be necessary to let some beans become overripe so that the majority are ripe enough for easy shelling. The overripe beans can be used in the same ways as dry beans.

—

Jalapeño Peppers see Peppers

—

Jerusalem Artichoke
Helianthus tuberosus

The Jerusalem artichoke is neither from Jerusalem nor an artichoke; it is a relative of the sunflower. It is an edible, crunchy round tuber about one-fourth the size of a large potato. The plant forms stalks that reach 6 to 8 feet in height and has 3-inch, sunflower-like blooms. Jerusalem artichokes are perennials hardy to −10° F but are grown as annuals because they become invasive if they are left in the garden.

Selected varieties

There are no named varieties of Jerusalem artichoke; it is sold under its common name. The artichokes mature in 110 days from root cuttings to tubers.

Growing conditions

Jerusalem artichokes sprout from the eyes—seeds embedded in small indentations—in their own tubers. Small tubers can be planted whole; large tubers should be cut into pieces that have at least one growing eye. In spring, cuttings should be planted 4 to 6 inches deep and 12 inches apart. If flower buds form on the plant, they should be removed before they blossom to encourage root growth.

Soil should be dry and sandy. Fertilize very sparingly and water only when the ground is dry.

Jerusalem artichoke is free of insects and diseases.

Harvesting

In the late fall, remove the tubers from the ground by digging a large, circular hole around each stalk, then lifting them from the soil by hand. Remove all of the tubers to prevent the plant from becoming an invasive weed.

—

Kidney Beans see Dry Beans

—

Leeks
Allium ampeloprasum,
Porrum Group

Leeks are members of the onion family with a mild, delicate, sweet flavor. Unlike onions, leeks do not form bulbs, but grow into thick, cylindrical, edible stalks that can reach 18 inches tall. The foliage, which is dark green, flat and straplike, can also be used in cooking.

Selected varieties

'Broad London,' 150 days from seed to mature root. Also called

'Large American Flag.' Blue-green leaves top thick, 9-inch-long stems. Tolerates cold; the best variety if plants will remain in the garden through winter. *'Titan,'* 110 days. Stalks are longer and thicker than those of *'Broad London,'* with slightly bulbous bases.

Growing conditions
Leeks are grown from seeds. Because they take a long time to mature, leek seeds are usually started indoors six to 10 weeks before transplanting into the garden. Germination takes about 10 days. The seedlings can be transplanted when they are about the thickness of a pencil; they should be spaced 3 to 6 inches apart.

Soil for leeks must be fertile, rich and constantly moist to ensure stem development. The soil pH must be in the 6.0 to 8.0 range. Fertilize at planting time with 5-10-5, and again when the tops are 6 to 9 inches tall.

It is possible to leave leeks in the ground over winter and harvest them the following spring. When this is done, apply mulch or some other winter protection if the temperature drops below 10° F.

Leeks are susceptible to damage from aphids and maggots; they are relatively disease-free.

Harvesting
Leeks can be harvested in the fall any time after they have reached ¾ inch in diameter; but if they are allowed to grow to 1½ inches in diameter, they will have a sweeter flavor. In areas with mild climates, leeks can be left in the ground all winter and harvested as needed, or harvested the following spring.

Lettuce
Lactuca sativa

What would a salad be without lettuce? Although several other greens are used as salad bases, lettuce is still the number one choice for salads.

There are four types of lettuce: butterhead, crisphead, leaf and romaine (also called cos). Butterhead lettuce has crisp, fleshy, delicate leaves of light to dark green that form a small, loose head; the interior of the head is creamy in color. Crisphead, also called iceberg lettuce, has a tight, firm head of brittle leaves. Since the plants cannot be crowded and are slow to mature, this is the most difficult type of lettuce to grow. Leaf lettuce is a nonheading lettuce with rumpled, frilled or oaklike leaves of light to dark green or bronze-red. It matures quickly and is the easiest lettuce to grow. Romaine lettuce has an upright, cylindrical head with firmly wrapped leaves that are light to medium green with a cream-colored interior. Romaine leaves have a slightly sweeter flavor than leaf or butterhead varieties.

Although lettuce is grown in summer, it does not do well in hot weather or warm soil. High temperatures can make lettuce bolt, meaning the plant produces flowers, which causes the leaves to wilt and become very bitter. Some types and varieties are less prone to bolting than others *(see below).* Generally, leaf and romaine types are the most heat-resistant.

Butterhead varieties
'Bibb,' 57 days from seed to mature head. Small heads of loosely folded, dark green leaves sometimes tinged with brown. Very little bitterness, even in outer leaves. Resistant to tip burn. *'Buttercrunch,'* 65 days. Thick, juicy, dark green, crumpled leaves form a compact head. This variety stays sweet even in hot weather and is very slow to bolt.

'Dark Green Boston,' 70 days. Tightly folded heads are made of smooth, tender, dark green leaves. *'Kagran Summer,'* 58 days. Thick leaves are medium green, forming an open but firm heart. Developed

'BUTTERCRUNCH' BUTTERHEAD LETTUCE

'ICEBERG' CRISPHEAD LETTUCE

'BLACK SEEDED SIMPSON' LEAF LETTUCE

'RED SAILS' LEAF LETTUCE

to tolerate summer heat, it is the most bolt-resistant butterhead.

Crisphead varieties

'Great Lakes,' 90 days from seed to mature head. Large, erect, fringed outer leaves cover a firm, glistening head. Although it does best in cool weather, it will tolerate warm weather. Resistant to tip burn. 'Iceberg,' 85 days. Crisp, tender heads of silver-white are surrounded by light green, crinkled leaves with edges often tinged in brown. Tolerates some heat. Resistant to tip burn.

'Ithaca,' 72 days. The heads are large, smooth, deep green and very firm. Slow to bolt. Resistant to tip burn. 'Vanguard,' 90 days. Best hot-weather crisphead. Dark green outer leaves around a firm head. Resistant to tip burn.

Leaf varieties

'Black Seeded Simpson,' 45 days from seed to mature leaves. Broad, light green leaves are frilled, crinkled and very crisp. Fast-growing. Can tolerate heat. 'Grand Rapids,' 50 days. Light green, wavy, very frilled, crispy leaves grow in large bunches. Fast-growing. Resistant to tip burn. 'Green Ice,' 45 days. Dark, glossy green leaves are wavy and crinkled. One of the slowest leaf varieties to bolt.

'Oakleaf,' 46 days. Thin, light green, oak-shaped leaves are deeply notched, with a sweet taste and a delicate texture. Heat-resistant; leaves are slow to turn bitter in hot weather. 'Prizehead,' 48 days. Light green, crisp, crinkled leaves turn outward; the upper parts are tinged with red. Can tolerate heat. 'Red Sails,' 42 days. Ruffled and fringed red-bronze leaves form a compact, open head with a full center.

'Red Salad Bowl,' 50 days. Deeply notched, bronze-red leaves form a full rosette. The plant is heat-resistant, although the color is best in cool weather. 'Ruby,' 47 days. Light green, frilled, crinkled leaves with streaks of bright red. Heat-resistant. 'Salad Bowl,' 46 days. Round, bowl-shaped plant with large, lime green rosettes. Leaves are long, wavy and deeply lobed. Heat-resistant. 'Tango,' 45 days. Very dark green, deeply cut, pointed leaves look like endive and have a tangy taste.

Romaine varieties

'Parris Island,' 70 days from seed to mature leaves. Dark green, slightly crinkled leaves form a tight, erect, 10-inch head. Slow to bolt. Resistant to tip burn and tolerant of lettuce mosaic. 'Valmaine,' 70 days. Large, upright, crinkled, dark green leaves. Slow to bolt. Resistant to downy mildew.

Growing conditions

Lettuce can be grown from seed or from purchased seedlings. Leaf lettuce is almost always grown from seed because it matures quickly. Butterhead and romaine varieties can be grown from either seed or seedlings. Crisphead lettuce requires a longer growing season and is almost always grown from purchased seedlings.

When lettuce is planted in spring, it should be done as soon as the ground can be worked; lettuce does better in cool temperatures. For a continuous harvest, lettuce can be planted successively every two weeks until hot weather arrives. After the high heat of summer is past, lettuce can be planted again if there is enough time for it to mature between planting and the first fall frost date. In mild-climate areas, lettuce can be planted throughout the winter.

Lettuce can be started from seeds sown indoors or directly in the garden; in either case, the seeds should not be covered with soil because they need light to germinate. To start crisphead varieties indoors, sow seeds 10 weeks before the last frost date; butterhead and romaine varieties need only six weeks before transplanting. Or, after the last frost, sow seeds directly in the soil, 3 inches apart. Germination takes seven to 10 days. Thin leaf lettuce to 6 inches apart, butterhead and romaine to 10 inches apart, crisphead to 12 inches apart. The thinnings can be used in salads and cooking.

Soil for lettuce must be neutral in pH, fertile and well drained. Soil must be kept uniformly and constantly moist, or the head-lettuce varieties will develop pinkish brown interiors. Fertilize before planting and again every three weeks to promote fast growth, which enhances the flavor. Frequent weeding is necessary; lettuce does not compete well with weeds. Mulch will reduce weed growth and keep the soil cool and moist.

Lettuce plants can be damaged by slugs and snails, aphids, mosaic, downy mildew and tip burn.

Harvesting
Leaves of leaf varieties can be picked from the outside of the plant any time they are large enough. With butterhead and romaine, outer leaves may be picked or the entire plant can be lifted from the soil when it matures. Crisphead lettuce is harvested when the center is firm; squeeze the head to test for firmness.

—

Lima Beans
Phaseolus limensis

Two types of lima beans are grown in home gardens: large-seeded and baby limas, also called butter beans. Both types are flat, light-colored beans from ½ to 1 inch long and have a mealy or nutlike flavor. Both are shelled before eating. Lima beans are available in both bush and pole varieties, but all baby limas grow on bush-type plants. The pole varieties mature later but bear over a longer period of time than the bush varieties.

Most of the northern part of the United States is not suited for growing the large-seeded limas; these beans need a long growing season of high temperatures. The baby limas mature faster and can be planted in areas where the growing season is short. Baby limas are also a good crop for the hot regions of the South and West because they are more heat-resistant than large-seeded varieties.

Bush varieties
'Dixie Butterpea,' 75 days from seed to mature bean. A round, white, meaty bean on a strong, vigorous plant. Tolerates heat and drought. *'Fordhook 242,'* 75 days. A large-seeded lima. High-yielding plant produces many pods with three or four plump, thick beans. Resistant to heat and rot. *'Geneva,'* 85 days. A baby lima. Small, buttery beans are light green. Seeds can germinate in cool soil, which gives the plant a longer growing season than other varieties.

'Henderson's Bush,' 65 days. Plant produces dark green, flat, 3-inch pods containing three or four creamy white, flat beans. *'Jackson Wonder,'* 65 days. Small buff-colored beans are mottled with purple. Plant and pods resemble *'Henderson's Bush,'* but are more heat- and drought-resistant.

Pole varieties
'Florida Butter,' 90 days from seed to mature bean. Light buff-colored bean splashed with purple produced on an 8- to 10-foot vine. Tolerates summer heat. *'King of the Garden,'* 88 days. Pods are 5 inches long and an inch wide; they contain three or four large, flat beans.

'Prizetaker,' 90 days. The largest lima bean. Pods grow at least 6 inches long, 1½ inches wide, and contain four or five beans. *'Sieva,'* 78 days. Also called *'Carolina.'* Fast-growing. Small, smooth, flat beans are medium green when fresh, white when dry.

Growing conditions
Lima beans are grown from seeds

'PARRIS ISLAND' ROMAINE LETTUCE

'FORDHOOK 242' BUSH LIMA BEAN

'KING OF THE GARDEN' POLE LIMA BEAN

'ANNIE OAKLEY' OKRA

sown directly in the soil because they do not transplant well. Sow the seeds in the spring, when the soil is 70° F or warmer. If the soil is cool, use a fungicide to prevent seeds from rotting.

Plant seeds 1 inch deep in clay soils and 1½ inches deep in sandy soils. Germination takes seven days. Thin both bush and pole varieties to about 8 inches apart.

Bush limas can be planted in succession every two weeks until approximately two months before the first fall frost. Pole lima beans will require staking; stake them as soon as the plants begin to develop so that they do not become tangled and damaged.

Soil should be light and well drained and have a pH higher than 6.0. Fertilize with 5-10-10 before planting but do not feed again during the season.

Lima beans are susceptible to damage from aphids, leafhoppers, mites, anthracnose, blight and mildew. Pole varieties are especially susceptible to damage from the bean beetle.

Harvesting

Beans can be picked as soon as pods are full-sized, between 3 and 5 inches long. Harvest pole lima beans carefully to prevent the vines from breaking; hold the vine in one hand while harvesting with the other. Pods should be picked as they mature to keep the plant productive. Late in the season, some limas can be left on the plant and harvested as dry beans.

—

Navy Beans see Dry Beans

New Zealand Spinach
see Summer Spinach

—

Okra
Hibiscus esculentus

Okra is a fast-growing plant that ranges from 3 to 8 feet in height and produces attractive, yellow, hollyhock-like blooms that have maroon centers. The flowers grow into slender, pointed, edible green seedpods up to 8 inches long. Their skin is either smooth or ribbed. The leaves are large, lush and lobed.

Selected varieties
'*Annie Oakley*,' 52 days from seed to ripe fruit. Compact plant produces long, slender pods; pods remain tender even if they are left on the plant longer than their maturity date. A good choice for areas where the climate is cool. Hybrid. '*Clemson Spineless*,' 56 days. Compact, 4-foot plant produces slim, slightly grooved, tapered, medium green pods.

'*Dwarf Green Long Pod*,' 52 days. Plant grows to only 3 feet tall. Pods are slim, slightly ridged, tapered and dark green. '*Emerald*,' 58 days. Tall plants produce smooth, round, slender, emerald green pods. '*Perkins Mammoth*,' 50 days. Plants grow to 5 feet tall; dark green pods remain tender even up to 8 inches long.

Growing conditions
Okra is started from seed. In warm areas with a long growing season, the seeds can be sown directly in the soil; they should be planted ½ to ¾ inch deep. In areas with a short growing season, the seeds can be started indoors four to six weeks before the last frost date. Germination takes 10 to 14 days. Thin the seedlings to 12 inches apart for the shorter varieties and 18 inches apart for the taller ones.

Okra will grow in any average clay soil with a neutral pH. Fertilize with 5-10-5 when the plants are 8 inches tall, and again when pods start to form.

From time to time, some flowers may drop off a plant before producing pods. This can be caused by a sudden change in the weather and need not be a cause for concern as long as the plant is healthy.

Okra plants can be damaged by

cold winds and in windy areas may require some protection, such as a location behind a fence. The plants are also susceptible to damage from fusarium wilt, corn earworms and nematodes.

Harvesting

Although okra pods can grow to 8 inches in length, they should generally be picked when they are 2 to 3 inches long, or they will become tough and tasteless. Harvesting should be done every two or three days to keep the plant producing. After the first harvest, remove the bottom leaves from the plant; this will help keep it productive.

In regions of the South and West where summers are hot, plants can become extremely tall, which makes harvesting difficult. Tall plants can be cut down to 12 to 18 inches; they will resprout and continue to produce.

—

Onion

Allium cepa, Cepa Group

Whether it be green, red, purple, yellow or white, the onion is one of the mainstays of the kitchen. It can be eaten raw or cooked and used to season a variety of dishes.

Onions are categorized in two groups: bulbing onions and bunching onions. Bulbing onions are grown for the 1- to 5-inch edible bulbs that form at the base of 20-inch foliage shoots. These bulbs, available in a variety of colors, are enclosed in papery skins. Bunching onions have either small bulbs or no bulbs at all; they are grown for their edible, tubular, multiple green stems that grow to 12 inches tall. They are called bunching onions because the stems grow in a bunch from the base. They continue to divide and sprout new stems throughout the growing season. Both bulbing and bunching onions harvested at an immature stage are called scallions.

Bulbing varieties are classified as either long-day or short-day onions. This is a critical distinction based on their growth habits; long-day onions will form bulbs only during the long days of summer in the northern parts of the United States, and short-day onions will form bulbs only during the short days of winter or the shorter days that occur in summer in the South.

Bulbing varieties

'*Autumn Spice,*' 100 days from seed to mature sets *(see below)*. Long-day. A medium-sized, globe-shaped onion with flattened ends. Stores well. '*Bermuda,*' 185 days. Short-day. A large, somewhat flat onion with mild flavor, white flesh and amber skin. Does not store well.

'*Burgundy,*' 95 days. Short-day. The hamburger onion. Has flattened ends, red skin and flesh marked with white rings. Very sweet. '*Crystal Wax Pickling,*' 60 days. Neutral as to day length. The cocktail onion. Small, round, glistening white bulbs for pickling.

'*Early Yellow Globe,*' 100 days. Long-day. A medium-sized, firm onion with white flesh and yellow skin. Blight-resistant. '*Fiesta Hybrid,*' 110 days. Long-day. A yellow, globe-shaped, Spanish-type onion *(see below)* with a small neck. Very sweet.

'*Southport Red Globe,*' 110 days. Long-day. A medium-sized, solid, round onion with thick skin over purple-red flesh. Very sweet. Stores well. '*Southport White Globe,*' 108 days. Long-day. Medium-sized, round white onion. Can be harvested for use as a scallion after 65 days. Stores better than other white varieties. '*Stockton Red,*' 100 days. Medium-sized, round onion with thick, dark purple skin.

'*Sweet Sandwich,*' 110 days. Long-day. Medium-sized, flat to globe-shaped, yellow hybrid onion. Very sweet. Stores well; mildness

'STOCKTON RED' BULBING ONION

'WHITE SWEET SPANISH' BULBING ONION

'YELLOW SWEET SPANISH' BULBING ONION

'JAPANESE BUNCHING' ONION

increases with storage. *'Texas Grano 502,'* 170 days. Short-day. Large onion with yellow skin over white flesh. Does not store well.

'White Sweet Spanish,' 120 days. Long-day. Firm, pure white skin covers white flesh on a very large, globe-shaped onion. Can be harvested early for use as a scallion. Does not store well. *'Yellow Granax,'* 120 days. Short-day. Large, globe-shaped onion with yellow skin and firm, mild flesh. Does not store well.

'Yellow Sweet Spanish,' 120 days. Long-day. Very large, globe-shaped onion with golden yellow skin and white flesh. Does not store well.

Bunching varieties

'Beltsville Bunching,' 120 days from seed to mature stems. Mild flavor. This is the best bunching variety for hot areas. *'Evergreen Bunching,'* 120 days. Stems are longer and more slender than *'Beltsville'*. Hardy in winter. *'Japanese Bunching,'* 110 days. Long, slender green stems. Plant forms little or no bulb.

'White Lisbon,' 60 days. Stalks are long, clear and white; upright, bright green foliage. Cold-tolerant.

Growing conditions

Onions can be grown from seeds, transplants or sets. Sets are dry bulbs whose growth has been temporarily halted. These are usually long-day onions and are grown only in the northern regions of the United States.

Onions started from seeds are usually sown indoors 10 to 12 weeks before the last frost date. In areas with a long growing season, they can be sown directly in the soil, ¼ to ½ inch deep. Germination takes 10 to 14 days. Transplants and sets should be planted about 1 inch deep.

The final spacing for plants, regardless of how they were started, depends on the type of onion. Bulbing onions should be spaced a dis-

tance slightly larger than their ultimate diameter. Bunching onions and those grown for scallions should be spaced 2 to 3 inches apart.

The soil must be well drained, high in organic matter, fertile and loose. Onions do not grow well in clay soils. The soil pH should be as close to neutral as possible. Fertilize heavily at the time of planting and feed twice more during the growing season.

Bulbing onions may poke their way out of the soil as they grow. This is not a concern; in fact, the sunlight on the top of the onion will help increase the bulb size.

Onions can be damaged by neck rot, maggots and thrips.

Harvesting

Bunching onions and onions grown for scallions may be harvested as soon as they are large enough. Remove only half of the bunch at one time; this allows new shoots to form within four to six weeks. Bunching onions do not store well, so they should be harvested as needed. In general, the longer they remain in the ground, the more pungent they will be.

Bulbing onions are ready for harvesting when their tops begin to turn brown. To hasten ripening, bend the tops over gently without breaking them. Several days later, dig around the onions carefully with a spading fork and lift the bulbs from the soil. Leave them in the sun for a week, until their necks are dry.

For storage, you can braid the foliage of smaller onions together and hang the entire clump, or keep the onions in a mesh bag. If the latter is done, leave about 1 inch of the stem on the top of the bulb. Storage areas should be dark, dry, cool and well ventilated.

—

Parsnips
Pastinaca sativa

Parsnips are long, carrot-like, yellowish white roots with leafy tops of lacy green foliage. The root can grow to 12 inches long and to 3 inches thick at the shoulder. Compound-leaved foliage grows to 18 inches tall. Parsnips are biennials and can remain in the ground through winter, but plants not harvested until spring lose some flavor and tenderness.

Selected varieties
'*All American*,' 110 days from seed to ripe fruit. A very tapered parsnip that is shorter and broader at the shoulder than most varieties. '*Harris Model*,' 110 days. A medium-length root; this is the smoothest and whitest variety. '*Hollow Crown*,' 100 days. A long, smooth, tapered variety.

Growing conditions
Parsnips are grown from seeds sown directly in the soil in early spring, as soon as the soil can be worked. Sow the seeds ¼ to ½ inch deep, and sow them generously; only a small percentage will germinate. The seeds may take as long as 18 days to sprout. When the seedlings are 1 inch tall, thin them to about 5 inches apart.

Parsnip seeds are short-lived. They should be stored in the refrigerator until sowing, and they cannot be saved from one year to the next.

Parsnips need warm but not excessively hot temperatures, so they are not a good summer crop in hot regions of the South and West.

Soil for parsnips should be light, loose, slightly acid and evenly moist to prevent root distortion. Fertilize with 5-10-5 prior to planting and again every month during the growing season. Keep the area weeded; parsnips do not compete well with weeds.

Parsnips are susceptible to damage from aphids, beetles, leafhoppers and leaf miners.

Harvesting
Parsnips are harvested in fall after the first frost; freezing temperatures help make the root sweet.

Use a garden fork to loosen the soil around the plant and then pull the root out of the soil. Parsnips can be harvested all at once and stored over the winter or harvested as needed. If they remain in the soil in winter, a straw mulch will help keep the ground warm and make harvesting easy.

—

Peppers
Capsicum annuum

Peppers are among the most versatile vegetables; they can be used for slicing and eating raw, and for frying, pickling, stuffing or spicing. They are available in a wide variety of shapes, colors, sizes and tastes. Peppers form from small, white flowers on an attractive, bushy plant that grows between 20 and 30 inches tall and wide.

Pepper varieties are classified as either sweet or hot. Most bell-shaped peppers are sweet peppers, but not all of them are. Most long, thin, tapered peppers are hot peppers, but again, not all of them are. The color of the pepper has nothing to do with its spiciness; all peppers, even the familiar green bell pepper, will eventually turn red or gold if left on the plant.

Pimentos are the sweetest peppers; when dried, they are ground to make paprika. Hot peppers are the source of cayenne pepper and Tabasco sauce.

Sweet varieties
'*Bell Boy*,' 70 days from transplanting to ripe fruit. Shiny, deep green fruit turns red at maturity. A large, four-lobed bell pepper, 4½ by 3½ inches, with thick walls and a mild flavor. Resistant to drought and tobacco mosaic virus. Hybrid.

'*Better Belle*,' 65 days. A blocky, four-lobed medium green bell pepper with thick walls; 4½ by 3½ inches. Resistant to tobacco mosaic virus. Hybrid. '*Big Bertha*,' 72 days. The largest bell pepper; 7 by

'HARRIS MODEL' PARSNIP

'BETTER BELLE' SWEET PEPPER

115

'GOLDEN BELL' SWEET PEPPER

'ANAHEIM TMR23' HOT PEPPER

'LONG RED CAYENNE' HOT PEPPER

4 inches, with three or four lobes and thick green walls. A good choice for cool climates. Resistant to tobacco mosaic virus. Hybrid.

'California Wonder,' 75 days. A four-lobed green bell pepper with thick flesh; 4 by 3 inches. Good for stuffing. Nonhybrid. *'Canape,'* 62 days. A three-lobed, slightly tapered bell pepper with medium green, thick flesh and mild flavor. Pepper is 3½ by 2½ inches. Good for short growing seasons. Resistant to heat, drought and tobacco mosaic virus. Hybrid.

'Cubanelle,' 65 days. Pepper is 6 inches long, tapering from 2½ inches at the top, light yellow-green turning red at maturity. Plants are very bushy. Nonhybrid. *'Emerald Giant,'* 74 days. A very productive plant with blocky, 4-by-4-inch bell peppers. Nonhybrid. Resistant to tobacco mosaic virus.

'Golden Bell,' 68 days. A three- or four-lobed, blocky, slightly tapered bell pepper that changes from light green to deep gold at maturity. Hybrid. *'Golden Summer,'* 67 days. A pale, lime green pepper that turns gold at maturity. It is a blocky, thick-walled, 4½-by-3½-inch, four-lobed bell pepper. Hybrid. Resistant to tobacco mosaic virus.

'Gypsy,' 60 days. A compact plant produces 5½-by-3-inch, wedge-shaped fruits that, as they mature, change from light green to golden yellow and finally to red. The plant is eye-catching; the peppers are crisp and crunchy. Good in any climate, especially in areas with a short growing season. Hybrid. Resistant to tobacco mosaic virus.

'Keystone Resistant Giant #3,' 75 days. Plant produces 4½-by-3¾-inch dark green, blocky, four-lobed bell peppers. Nonhybrid. Tolerates high heat and resists tobacco mosaic virus. *'Patio Bell,'* 60 days. A stocky, compact plant, good for container growing, produces three- or four-lobed, blocky, green, thick-walled bell peppers. Hybrid. Tolerant to tobacco mosaic virus.

'Pimento,' 78 days. A heart-shaped, very sweet, mild, 3½-by-2-inch pepper. Nonhybrid. *'Pimento Perfection,'* Nonhybrid. Similar to *'Pimento'* but is more resistant to tobacco mosaic. *'Purple Belle,'* 75 days. This blocky, 3½-inch-square, four-lobed bell pepper turns from green to purple to red. Compact plant. Hybrid.

'Sweet Cherry,' 78 days. Also called *'Red Cherry Sweet.'* A small, slightly tapered pepper 1½ inches across. Good for pickling. Nonhybrid. *'Sweet Banana,'* 70 days. Also called *'Hungarian Sweet Wax.'* A waxy, tapered pepper 6 inches long and 1½ inches wide, with a light yellow color that turns red at maturity. Nonhybrid.

'Whopper Improved,' 71 days. Square, 4-inch bell pepper has four lobes. Hybrid. Resistant to tobacco mosaic virus. *'Yolo Wonder,'* 75 days. Plant produces 4-inch-square, glossy green bell peppers. Hybrid. Resistant to tobacco mosaic virus.

Hot varieties
'Anaheim TMR23,' 77 days from transplanting to ripe fruit. A long, tapered, flat pepper 8 by 2½ inches. One of the mildest hot peppers. Nonhybrid. *'Fire!'* 75 days. Extremely hot. Tapered pepper 2 inches by ½ inch. Nonhybrid. *'Hungarian Yellow Wax,'* 65 days. Also known as *'Hungarian Hot Wax'* and *'Hot Banana.'* Matures from canary yellow to bright red. Medium hot, 6 by 2 inches and tapered. Nonhybrid.

'Jalapa,' 65 days. An oval pepper tapering to a blunt tip, measuring 2½ inches by 1 inch. Hot. Compact plant. Hybrid. *'Jalapeño,'* 75 days. Cone-shaped, 3-by-1-inch pepper. Nonhybrid. *'Long Red Cayenne,'* 75 days. Curled and twisted pepper is 5 inches by ½ inch. Hot. Nonhybrid.

'Mexi Bell,' 70 days. A three- or

four-lobed bell pepper that is mildly hot. Hybrid. Resistant to tobacco mosaic virus. 'Red Cherry Hot,' 75 days. Round, 1½-inch pepper. Nonhybrid. 'Red Chili,' 80 days. A 2½-by-½-inch, tapered, very hot pepper. Nonhybrid.

'Roumanian Wax,' 65 days. Also called 'Roumanian Hot.' Yellow pepper turns red at maturity. Medium hot, 4 by 2½ inches and slightly blocky. Nonhybrid. 'Serrano Chili,' 75 days. Hot. Pepper is 2½ inches long, ½ inch across and rounded at the bottom.

'Tabasco' (Capsicum frutescens), 80 days. Slender, bullet-shaped, 2-by-½-inch, very hot pepper. Turns from green to yellow at maturity. Used to make Tabasco sauce. Nonhybrid.

Growing conditions
Peppers can be grown either from seeds or from purchased seedlings. Since peppers require a long, warm growing season, seeds are generally started indoors, eight to 10 weeks before transplanting. Seeds should be sown ⅛ inch deep. Germination takes 10 days. Transplanting can be done when temperatures are consistently in the 60s. The plants should be set 18 to 24 inches apart, so that they will just touch each other when mature.

Soil should be rich, moist, well drained and slightly acid. Do not overfertilize peppers; this will cause lush foliage growth and no fruit. Feed lightly at planting time and again in six weeks.

Pepper plants can be damaged by sunscald, tobacco mosaic virus, aphids, borers and cutworms.

Harvesting
The pepper is a unique plant because it will produce only a certain number of fruits at one time. Once that number is reached, the plant stops producing blossoms. When some of the fruits are harvested, the plant will resume production.

Sweet varieties are usually harvested when they are immature, green, full-sized and firm, but if they are allowed to mature and turn red on the vine, the peppers will be sweeter and higher in vitamins A and C. Hot varieties are picked after they have reached maturity. The fruit of both varieties can be cut or picked from the stem; in either case be sure to leave a piece of stem on the pepper.

—

Pimento see Peppers

Pinto Beans see Dry Beans

Popcorn see Corn

—

Potato
Solanum tuberosum

The potato is an edible underground tuber that forms between the base of an underground stem and the roots. Tubers can be either round or oblong, with brown or red skin and with white or cream-colored flesh. Varieties are classifed by the way they are to be cooked—boiled or baked. The flesh of the two types is different in texture; boiling varieties are moist and baking varieties are dry and mealy. The plant grows 30 inches high and 4 feet wide. Its flowers are pale pink to white with protruding yellow centers; leaves are large and compound. Potatoes are annuals.

Baking varieties
'Katahdin,' 115 days from seed potato to mature potato. Large, round to oblong potato with cream-colored skin. 'Kennebec,' 105 days. A large, hefty, oblong potato with smooth texture and white flesh. Good for baking and storage. Resistant to late blight. 'Russet Burbank,' 130 days. The oblong, cylindrical Idaho potato. 'White Cobbler,' 90 days. A very popular oblong baking potato. Good for short growing seasons. Does not store well.

'RED CHERRY HOT' PEPPER

'SERRANO CHILI' HOT PEPPER

'KATAHDIN' BAKING POTATO

'NORLAND' BOILING POTATO

Boiling varieties

'*Explorer*,' 100 days from seed to mature potato. A variety grown from true seed. Potatoes are small and creamy white. '*Norland*,' 90 days from seed potato to mature potato. Red-skinned potato with shallow eyes and smooth white flesh. Resistant to scab.

'*Red Pontiac*,' 100 days. Rosy red, thin skin covers white flesh. Smooth texture, good for boiling. Does well in heavy soil. '*Superior*,' 100 days. Potato is oval to round with smooth skin. Good for northern climates. Stores well.

Growing conditions

Although there are a few varieties of potato that are grown from true seed, the plant is most frequently grown from a seed potato— a portion of a mature potato that has at least one eye. The eye is a seed in an indentation on the potato skin. A new potato plant sprouts from it.

When you purchase seed potatoes, be sure they are certified disease-free by the state agricultural department. Although it is possible to grow plants from store-bought potatoes, it is not recommended because the risk of disease is high, and store-bought potatoes are usually treated with a sprout inhibitor.

Seed potatoes come in various sizes. The optimum seed potato is about 1½ by 2 inches in size, weighs 2 to 3 ounces and has one to three eyes. Larger seed potatoes need to be cut into blocks of roughly these dimensions; if you do so, be sure that each piece has at least one eye. The pieces should be placed in a light, airy location for one or two days to dry.

Plant seed potatoes in early spring about five weeks before the last frost. Set them 4 to 5 inches deep with the eyes facing up. Space them 12 to 15 inches apart.

If you grow potatoes from true seeds, start the seeds indoors six to eight weeks before the last frost date. Transplant the seedlings into the garden when all danger of frost has passed; use the same spacing as for seed potatoes.

Potatoes do best in mild, warm-summer climates. Since cool nights aid the final stages of the ripening process, potatoes are grown as fall and spring crops in hot regions of the South and West.

Soil must be sandy, rich in organic matter, well drained, loose and acid, with a pH between 4.5 and 5.5. At planting time, mix 5-10-5 into the soil before setting the potatoes in place. No further fertilizing is needed.

If you plant potatoes in the soil, as opposed to laying them under straw *(page 48)*, the soil must be tilled, or mounded up, around the potatoes to keep them from poking through the soil and being exposed to light. Light turns potatoes green, bitter and slightly poisonous. Any potatoes having a greenish cast should be discarded.

Potatoes can be damaged by the Colorado potato beetle, flea beetle, aphid, leafhopper, scab and blight.

Harvesting

Immature potatoes, also called new potatoes, are harvested in midsummer about the time the plants are in bloom. Harvest them by digging gently around the plant and removing some tubers, leaving the rest to grow to full size.

Mature potatoes are harvested in the fall, when the plant tops die back. Use a potato rake or a garden fork to loosen the soil first and minimize damage to the tubers; then gently lift out the potatoes.

Cure potatoes by storing them in a warm, dark place for 14 days; then move them to a cool—about 50° F—dry location.

Pumpkin
Cucurbita

This Halloween favorite is a member of the squash family. It grows on large, sprawling vines that can spread to 10 feet, and on bush-type plants that reach 3 feet in width. The plant stems are prickly. The leaves are large, triangular and slightly lobed. The yellow flowers develop into large round fruits with orange skin.

Pumpkins belong to one of two species. 'C. pepo,' the smaller, ranges from 6 to 20 pounds and is used for baking and carving. 'C. maxima,' the larger, ranges from 20 to 100 pounds and is grown primarily for exhibition. The varieties listed below are vining plants unless otherwise noted.

Selected varieties
'Big Max,' 120 days from seed to ripe fruit. A globe-shaped pumpkin that can grow to 100 pounds. The skin is rough and reddish pink; underneath is a layer of orange-yellow flesh that is 4 inches thick and stringy. Nonhybrid.

'Cinderella,' 95 days. A bush-type plant with globe-shaped, 10-inch fruit that has smooth, bright orange skin. Does not store well. Nonhybrid.

'Connecticut Field,' 100 days. Also called 'Big Tom.' One of the most popular mammoth varieties for carving. Rounded fruit is flat at both ends; grows to 25 pounds and 12 inches in diameter. Skin is hard, slightly ribbed and dark orange. Nonhybrid.

'Jack O' Lantern,' 110 days. An oval fruit 7 by 9 inches and up to 15 pounds. Smooth, medium bright orange skin and yellow flesh. Nonhybrid. 'Small Sugar,' 100 days. Also called 'New England Pie.' Globe-shaped fruit grows to 8 pounds and 7 inches across. Skin is deep orange and slightly ribbed; flesh is yellow-orange and firm. Nonhybrid.

'Spirit,' 90 days. A semibush plant that spreads to 6 feet. Fruit has bright orange skin and golden yellow flesh, grows to 12 inches in diameter and weighs as much as 15 pounds. Stores well. Hybrid.

'Triple Treat,' 110 days. So named because it is good in three ways; it can be carved, it can be baked and its hull-less seeds can be eaten. Round fruit, 7 to 9 inches across, weighs 6 to 8 pounds. Stores well. Hybrid.

Growing conditions
Pumpkins are grown from seeds sown directly in the soil in spring after all danger of frost has passed. The seeds should be sown ½ to 1 inch deep. Germination takes seven to 10 days.

Although pumpkin seedlings generally do not transplant well, they can be started indoors if the seeds are planted in individual peat pots that can go with them into garden soil and thus reduce transplant shock. Pumpkin seeds should be started four or five weeks before the last frost date and planted outdoors after all danger of frost has passed.

Sow seeds either in groups in mounded hills or in rows. Space the hills 6 to 8 feet apart for vining plants and 3 to 4 feet apart for bush plants. Plant four to six seeds per hill. After germination, thin the hills to two plants per hill. If seeds are sown in rows, space the seeds 6 inches apart. After germination, thin vining plants to 4 feet apart and bush plants to 3 feet apart.

Soil for pumpkins must be rich in organic matter, well drained and have a neutral pH. Fertilize with 5-10-5 at planting time and again every four weeks until harvest. Pumpkins are among the few summer vegetables that will tolerate light shade.

Approximately one month before harvest, pinch back any new tips and remove the smaller fruits from the plant so the largest pumpkins can develop to full size.

To raise large, exhibition pumpkins, select one of the large-fruited varieties and allow only one pumpkin to develop on the plant.

Pumpkins can be damaged by vine borers and cucumber beetles.

'BIG MAX' PUMPKIN

'VALENTINE' RHUBARB

Harvesting

As pumpkins mature, they should be raised off the ground on boards to prevent the bottoms from rotting *(page 70)*. Pumpkins are harvested in the fall, when the rind becomes hard and the foliage starts to die. They will tolerate light frost but must be harvested before a hard frost. Leave a piece of the stem on the pumpkin to prevent rotting.

—

Rhubarb

Rheum rhabarbarum

Rhubarb is usually grown for its edible stalks, which are used to make tart-flavored pies, preserves and sauces. It is also an attractive plant with colorful foliage, and it is often planted in perennial borders for its ornamental value. Its green, pink or red leaf stalks grow from 18 to 26 inches high and to 2 inches thick. The leaves are heart-shaped, textured, curled and deep green tinged with red. Though attractive, the leaves are poisonous and should be stripped from the stalks when they are harvested.

Selected varieties

'*Cherry*' has red stalks. Good for mild-winter areas as it needs less winter cold than other varieties. '*MacDonald*' has bright red stalks. '*Valentine*' has deep red stalks that retain their color when cooked. The sweetest variety. '*Victoria*' has green stalks that are sometimes tinged with pink. This variety is usually started from seed.

Growing conditions

Rhubarb can be grown only in areas with cold winters and mild summers. It must have at least two months of freezing temperatures in order to produce and does not tolerate temperatures above 90° F.

Rhubarb is generally grown from root divisions. It can be started from seed, but this is risky, since a plant grown from seed may not grow true to the variety, is not as strong as a plant started from a root division and takes longer to mature.

To start rhubarb from seeds, sow directly in the soil in early spring. Plant the seeds 1 inch deep and 6 inches apart. Germination will take 12 to 14 days. Thin the seedlings to 12 inches apart. In the second year, thin or transplant them to 36 inches apart.

Root divisions may be either purchased at a garden center or taken from old plants in your own or a friend's garden. The plants should be divided every four years or when stalks start to grow thin. Early spring is the best time for dividing. Cut the roots of old plants into clumps, each of which has at least one bud, or eye—a whitish, red-tinted protrusion pointing upward from the root. Plant the clumps 36 inches apart, with the eye set 3 inches deep in the soil.

Soil should be neutral, moist, well drained and rich in organic matter. Incorporate 5-10-5 into the soil before planting. After the first year, feed plants in spring, when growth starts, and again in fall, after harvest. Add mulch for protection during winter in areas where temperatures drop below 10° F.

Rhubarb plants can be damaged by slugs, snails, earwigs, beetles or leaf spot.

Harvesting

Stalks should not be harvested for at least one year after plants are grown from root cuttings or for two years after plants are started from seeds. Outer stalks can be harvested in spring and early summer when they are 18 to 24 inches long. Pull or break them off at the base instead of cutting them, because cutting may damage the roots located at the soil surface. Any stalks less than 1 inch thick should be left on the plant.

Rhubarb can be harvested over a six- to eight-week period. Do not at any time remove more than half of the plant's stalks; some foliage is necessary to strengthen the plant and encourage future growth.

—

Salsify
Tragapogon porrifolius

Salsify is grown for its 8-inch, tapered, smooth, thick taproot, which in its appearance resembles a parsnip, with dull, creamy white flesh. Because it tastes something like an oyster, salsify is also called oyster plant or vegetable oyster. The foliage looks like clumps of thick grass.

Selected varieties
'Sandwich Island Mammoth,' 120 days from seed to mature root. The most widely available variety.

Growing conditions
Salsify is started from seeds sown directly in the soil about two weeks before the last spring frost. The seeds should be sown ¼ inch deep and 2 inches apart. Germination takes seven days. When the plant tops are 3 inches high, the plants should be thinned to about 5 inches apart.

Soil must be light, sandy, deep and rich in organic matter—but manure should not be used because it causes the roots to split. The roots also crack in dry soil; soil should be kept moist. Fertilize with 5-10-5 at planting time and again in two months.

Salsify is generally insect- and disease-free; but if aphids or tarnished plant bugs are in the garden, they may attack salsify plants.

Harvesting
Dig up the roots in fall, just before the ground freezes. Soaking the soil first will make the roots easier to remove. Some roots can also be left in the ground all winter and then harvested in spring.

—

Scallion see Onion

Shallot
Allium cepa, Aggregatum Group

Shallot is the onion substitute called for in many French gourmet recipes; it has a more delicate, subtle flavor than the standard onion.

The plant is grown primarily for its bulb, which is shaped like garlic but is smaller and chestnut brown rather than white. Each bulb may have three to four cloves. The foliage is also edible; it resembles immature green onions with long, tube-shaped leaves.

Selected varieties
Shallot has no specific varieties; it is sold under its common name. It develops in 90 days from clove to mature bulb.

Growing conditions
The shallot grows from a bulb, which can be purchased from a garden supply store or from a gourmet market. The bulb should be broken into separate cloves. Each clove is inserted into the soil so that the tip is just below the soil surface. Cloves should be spaced about 3 inches apart.

The cloves can be planted in early spring, as soon as the soil can be worked. In the hot South and West, they can be planted in the fall for harvest the following spring.

Soil should be loose and rich with a neutral pH. Add a low-nitrogen fertilizer such as 5-10-10 to the soil at planting time. Feed again halfway through the growing season.

Shallots are generally insect- and disease-free but may be attacked by aphids and maggots.

Harvesting
Young shallots can be harvested and used like green onions. To harvest full-sized bulbs, wait until fall, when the foliage starts to turn brown. To encourage the bulb to ripen, bend the foliage down without breaking it off. After five days, dig up the bulbs and store them in a cool, airy, dry spot.

After harvesting, save sever-

'SANDWICH ISLAND MAMMOTH' SALSIFY

SHALLOT

'ROMANO' BUSH BEAN

'ROMANO' POLE BEAN

al bulbs for cloves to start next year's crop.

—

Snap Beans
Phaseolus vulgaris

Snap beans are pods of seeds harvested before the seeds mature. Most varieties of snap beans are green and are also called green beans, French beans or string beans. Very few of them are true string beans. This is a name once given to the bean because the seam of the pod used to have a string that needed to be removed before cooking, a nuisance eliminated by modern breeding. Some varieties of snap beans are yellow; these are also called wax beans. A few varieties are purple.

Snap beans are oval, round, or broad and flat pods ranging from 5 to 12 inches long. They grow on one of two types of plants: bush plants and vines. The vine types are also called pole beans because they must be supported. Bush varieties are full, stocky plants that grow to 20 inches tall. The plants produce beans for only about three weeks; for a continuous supply, they must be planted successively every two to three weeks. Pole varieties grow 6 to 8 feet tall. Once they mature, they produce beans over a period of about eight weeks.

Whether you select bush beans or pole beans will depend on how you intend to use the crop. Bush beans mature over a concentrated period of time, which is an advantage if you can or freeze them. Pole beans grow more slowly and produce more pods over a longer period of time, which is preferable if you want to eat them fresh.

Bush varieties
'Blue Lake,' 57 days from seed to ripe bean. Smooth, medium green, round, 6-inch pods with white seeds on a 16-inch plant. The entire crop matures at once. Resistant to common bean mosaic. 'Brittle Wax,' 52 days. A high-yielding wax bean plant. The pod is lemon yellow, rounded, slightly curved and 7 inches long. 'Cherokee Wax,' 52 days. Bright yellow, straight or slightly curved pods up to 6 inches long. Resistant to common bean mosaic.

'Contender,' 49 days. Dark green beans that are oval, slim, slightly curved and 6 inches long with buff seeds. The plant tolerates both hot and cold weather and is resistant to powdery mildew and common bean mosaic. 'Goldcrop,' 45 days. Yellow, rounded, straight pods 6 inches long with white seeds. The most disease-resistant variety of wax bean.

'Greencrop,' 55 days. Flat, dark green pods are 6½ inches long and straight; seeds are white. Tolerant of mildew and common bean mosaic. 'Greensleeves,' 56 days. Dark green pods are straight, rounded, thick and smooth; seeds are white. Resistant to common bean mosaic. 'Honey Gold,' 40 days. Short, round and straight pods are gold on a 14-inch plant. Resistant to common bean mosaic.

'Romano,' 53 days. Also known as 'Roma II.' This is the bush form of the 'Romano' pole bean. The bush variety matures earlier and is more disease-resistant. Flat green pods are 4 inches long and filled with buff seeds. Flavor is stronger and sharper than other varieties'. Resistant to common bean mosaic and mildew. 'Royal Burgundy,' 51 days. Purple-podded, 5-inch beans turn green when cooked, making them an excellent indicator for blanching. Good in cool soil.

'Tendercrop,' 53 days. Medium green pods are smooth, slim, round and 5 inches long with a pointed tip. Flavor is crisp. Seed is mottled purple. Resistant to common bean mosaic. 'Tenderpod,' 50 days. Deep green, meaty pods are round, thick, 5 inches long and tender. 'Top Crop,' 50 days. Vigorous, straight to slightly curved, 6-inch, round pods. Resistant to common bean mosaic.

Pole varieties

'Blue Lake,' 60 days from seed to ripe bean. Rounded, dark green, straight pods to 6 inches long. Seeds are white. Plant is high-yielding. Resistant to common bean mosaic. *'Golden,'* 60 days. Flat, yellow wax beans are 1 inch wide. Pods are 6 inches long. *'Kentucky Wonder,'* 65 days. Vigorous, high-yielding plant. Pods are 8 inches long, straight, smooth and oval with a meaty taste.

'Oregon Giant,' 65 days. Green pods grow to 12 inches long. *'Romano,'* 65 days. Also called Italian bean. A distinctive, broad, flat pod to 5 inches long. *'Royalty,'* 53 days. Bright purple, slightly curved pods grow to 5 inches long. Seeds are buff-colored. This variety will germinate in cooler soil than most beans. Its runners are short and generally do not need staking.

'Scarlet Runner Bean,' (Phaseolus coccineus), 65 days. A vegetable that is frequently grown for its ornamental value. The vine grows to 15 feet. Its scarlet blossoms are attractive. The pods grow to 12 inches long. Can be grown as a perennial where winter temperatures do not drop below 20° F.

Growing conditions

Snap beans are grown from seeds sown directly in the soil in spring, when the ground is warm and all danger of frost has passed. Seeds should be sown 1 inch deep in heavy soil and 1½ inches deep in sandy soil. Germination will take six days. White-seeded beans may not germinate as well as others and thus should be sown more heavily than other varieties.

The spacing for bush beans should be 3 to 4 inches between plants, except for the flat-podded varieties, which require slightly more space. The spacing for pole beans depends on the type of support used. In general, several seeds should be sown at the base of each support and then thinned to keep only the strongest seedling per support.

Beans do best in areas with warm summers, but they will not produce in extreme heat. In the South and West, beans are generally grown as spring and fall crops. Bush beans are more heat- and drought-resistant than pole beans.

Beans will grow in any average, well-drained garden soil with a pH of over 6.0. Fertilize prior to planting with 5-10-10; no further feeding will be needed.

Bean plants can be damaged by mosaic, rust, anthracnose, blight, powdery mildew, aphids, bean beetles, leafhoppers and mites.

Harvesting

Snap beans can be harvested when they are large enough to eat; the seeds should be starting to fill out. Hold the plant stem in one hand while pulling the pods off with the other; do not let the stem break.

—

Sorrel
Rumex acetosa

Sorrel, also called sour grass, is grown for its tart, tangy, citrus-flavored leaves, which are used in soups and salads. Its arrow-shaped foliage, 8 to 16 inches long and high in vitamin C, grows on upright plants in large, dense clumps. When in bloom, the plants can reach 4 feet in height, but without flowers they are 18 inches high. Although sorrel is a perennial hardy to −20° F in winter, it is generally grown as an annual because it becomes invasive.

Selected varieties

Although a few varieties of sorrel have been developed, sorrel is most often sold under its common name. The plants mature in 100 days from seed to ripe leaves.

'SCARLET RUNNER' BEAN

SORREL

'CALIFORNIA BLACKEYE' SOUTHERN PEA

'PINKEYE PURPLE HULL' SOUTHERN PEA

Growing conditions

Sorrel is usually grown from seeds planted directly in the soil in spring. Seeds should be sown ⅛ inch deep and 4 inches apart. After germination, which takes 10 days, the plants should be thinned to 10 inches apart. If sorrel is left in the ground and grown as a perennial, new plants can be started from root divisions of old plants. Because sorrel is a rapid spreader, it can be divided every two to three years.

Although sorrel will grow in areas of high heat, its flavor is best when it matures in cool temperatures. It is one of the relatively few vegetables that will tolerate partial shade.

Soil should be well drained and have a neutral pH; acid soil encourages the weedy characteristics of the plant. To help control its invasiveness, cut off the flower heads as soon as they appear so seeds will not spread.

Sorrel plants are susceptible to slug and snail damage.

Harvesting

Individual leaves can be cut from the plant as needed, or the entire plant can be cut off at ground level and the leaves removed. If sorrel is grown as a perennial, it can be cut to the ground after spring harvest and allowed to regrow for harvest in the fall.

—

Southern Peas
Vigna unguiculata

Southern peas, also called black-eyed peas or cowpeas, are legumes, like beans; they are called peas because the seeds are round. The plant grows to 24 inches tall. Most varieties are erect and bushy, but a few are sprawling with short runners. The pods are either slender or plump and smooth or lumpy, depending on the variety. They splay out like fingers above shiny, dark green leaves on long, smooth stems. The beans are white, cream or purple and from ½ to ⅜ inch long. They can be harvested and shelled when mature or left on the plant to be used as dry beans.

Selected varieties
'*California Blackeye,*' 75 days from seed to ripe bean. Large, smooth, 8-inch pods are filled with white beans that have black eyes, or spots. Resistant to wilt and nematodes. '*Crimson,*' 75 days. Green pods streaked with red are 7 inches long and grow above the foliage. Beans are light brown in color. '*Mississippi Silver,*' 65 days. Smooth pods are green with a silver sheen and are sometimes streaked with pink. '*Pinkeye Purple Hull,*' 78 days. Slender, rounded, deep purple pods to 8 inches long. White seeds have small purple eyes. '*Yardlong*' *(V. u. sesquipedalis),* 75 days. Also called asparagus bean. Robust vines reach 6 to 8 feet and produce slender, round, green pods that can grow up to 3 feet long.

Growing conditions

Southern peas are grown from seeds planted directly in the soil after all danger of frost has passed and soil is 70° F. Seeds should be sown from ½ to 1 inch deep depending on the soil; heavier soils call for a shallower planting depth. Germination takes 10 days. The percentage of germination is not high, so seeds should be sown generously. Seedlings should be thinned to 6 inches apart.

Southern peas do well in heat and drought, and are a good crop to grow where it is too hot for snap beans. Soil should be average to rich and well drained. Fertilize prior to planting with 5-10-10 and do not fertilize again.

Southern peas can be damaged by anthracnose, blight, powdery mildew, aphids, bean beetles, leafhoppers, mites and nematodes.

Harvesting
Individual pods can be picked for

shelling as they mature. The beans will expand and form lumps within the pod. The pods will change color. Some of the pods may be left on the plant and harvested later for dry beans.

—

Soybeans
Glycine max

Soybean plants are 3 feet tall, bushy and erect with round, furry leaves. They produce short, hairy pods that cling close to the stem. Each pod contains two or three round, pea-sized, black or yellow beans. Soybeans are rich in fat and have three times the protein of other beans.

Selected varieties
'*Prize*,' 85 days from seed to ripe shell bean. Plant produces two to four yellow beans per pod.

Growing conditions
Sow soybeans directly in the soil in spring, after all danger of frost has passed and the soil is warm. In sandy soil, sow the seeds 2 inches deep; in heavy soil, sow them 1 inch deep. Seeds will germinate within 12 days. Thin the seedlings to 4 inches apart.

Soybeans do well in areas with a long, hot growing season. Soybeans thrive in almost any soil, but they are not drought-resistant and should be watered regularly. Fertilize the soil with 5-10-10 before planting and do not feed the plants again. Although soybeans are erect, bushy plants, they will need some sort of a support if they are planted in a windy area.

Soybeans can be damaged by anthracnose, blight, mosaic, powdery mildew, aphids, bean beetles, mites and leafhoppers.

Harvesting
Soybeans can be picked for shelling when they are full-sized, plump and still green. Beans may also be left on the plant so that they can be harvested when they are dry.

—

Spinach see Summer Spinach

Squash see Summer Squash; Winter Squash

String Beans see Snap Beans

—

Summer Spinach
Tetragonia tetragonioides

True spinach cannot be grown in summer heat, but New Zealand spinach, also called summer spinach, is a warm-weather spinach substitute. It has triangular, dark green, shiny leaves that are thick and succulent and have a flavor similar to spinach. The plant is bushy; in cool climates, it produces runners that form a dense mat 2 to 3 feet wide, and in warm climates the runners grow to several feet long and can be trained on a trellis. Slender clusters of tiny yellow flowers appear above the foliage.

Selected varieties
There are no named varieties of New Zealand spinach; it is sold under its common name. The spinach matures in 60 days from seed to ripe leaves.

Growing conditions
New Zealand spinach is usually started from seeds sown directly in the soil in spring, after all danger of frost has passed. The seeds are planted 1 inch deep and 12 inches apart. Germination takes eight days. As a seed is actually a small fruit containing two or three seeds, thinning must be done soon after germination. When the plants are 4 inches tall, they should be thinned again to stand 18 inches apart.

Seeds can also be started indoors; but since they do not transplant well, they should be sown in individual peat pots that can go with

'PRIZE' SOYBEAN

NEW ZEALAND SPINACH

'EARLY GOLDEN SUMMER' CROOKNECK SQUASH

'SUNBURST HYBRID' SCALLOP SQUASH

'BUTTERSTICK HYBRID' STRAIGHTNECK SQUASH

them into the garden to reduce transplant shock. They can be started 6 weeks before the last frost date and then, when all danger of frost has passed, planted in the garden 18 inches apart.

Soil should be an average, sandy garden loam. Fertilize with 5-10-5 before planting and once again in midsummer. The plant is heat- and drought-resistant and can be grown as a perennial in mild climates.

New Zealand spinach is resistant to most insects and diseases.

Harvesting

Pick off new and tender leaves from the tips of the branches about once a week to keep the plant producing new foliage.

—

Summer Squash
Cucurbita pepo

Squash is among the most commonly homegrown vegetables and it does well in almost all of the United States. It is a space-consuming, bushy plant that spreads to 3 feet and has large, dark green leaves. Fruit may be round or oblong with white, yellow, green or orange edible flesh and skin.

There are four types of summer squash varieties: crookneck, scallop, straightneck and zucchini. Crookneck varieties have tapering bodies and curved necks. Scallop varieties are round and bowl-shaped with scalloped edges. Straightneck varieties are long and tapering without distinctive necks. Zucchini varieties are straight, cylindrical fruits with yellow, gray, green or black skin.

The types listed below are standard varieties except where noted.

Crookneck varieties
'Dixie,' 45 days from seed to ripe fruit. Compact plant. Fruit has smooth, lemon yellow skin and a thick neck. Hybrid. 'Early Golden Summer,' 53 days. Small fruit with warted, bright yellow skin.

'Pic-N-Pic,' 50 days. Golden yellow fruit with smooth, wart-free skin. Hybrid. 'Sundance,' 52 days. Fruit has a medium-thick neck, smooth, bright yellow skin and pale yellow flesh. Hybrid. 'Tara,' 51 days. Butter yellow fruit is 3 to 4 inches long and has a slender neck. Hybrid.

Scallop varieties
'Early White Bush Scallop,' 60 days from seed to ripe fruit. Also called 'White Patty Pan.' Pale green, flat fruit, creamy white flesh. One of the largest squash plants. 'Patty Green Tint,' 50 days. Light green flattened fruit. Hybrid. 'Peter Pan Hybrid,' 50 days. Light green fruit with meaty flesh. Matures earlier than most scallop varieties. 'Scallopini,' 50 days. Semibush plant. Dark green fruit to 3 inches in diameter. 'Sunburst Hybrid,' 53 days. Bright, golden yellow fruit is lightly scalloped and has a green sunburst pattern at both ends. Buttery taste. Firm but tender flesh.

Straightneck varieties
'Butterstick Hybrid,' 50 days from seed to ripe fruit. Evenly tapered golden fruit with creamy white flesh of firm texture and a sweet, nutty flavor. 'Early Prolific Straight,' 50 days. Bushy plant bears cream-colored fruit that grows to 6 inches long. 'Goldbar,' 53 days. Smooth, golden yellow skin; fruit is cylindrical. Compact plant. Hybrid. 'Park's Creamy Hybrid,' 48 days. Cream- to tan-colored fruit grows to 8 inches long on plants 2 feet high.

Zucchini varieties
'Ambassador Hybrid,' 48 days from seed to ripe fruit. Smooth, dark green fruit, 7 to 8 inches long. 'Aristocrat,' 53 days. Dark green fruit on a compact plant. Hybrid. 'Black Jack,' 48 days. Fruit grows to 7 inches long and has dark green skin with pale green flecks. 'Burpee Hybrid,' 50 days. Medium green fruit with shiny skin on a bush-type plant. 'Cocozelle,' 60 days. Also

called Italian vegetable marrow. The skin has stripes of light and dark green. Fruit has firm flesh; grows to 8 inches long. *'Gold Rush,'* 50 days. Compact plant. Fruit grows to 8 inches long and has smooth, thin, golden yellow skin and white flesh. Hybrid.

'Golden Zucchini,' 54 days. Glossy, bright golden skin. Long, slender, cylindrical fruit. *'Richgreen Hybrid,'* 50 days. Glossy, dark green skin. Fruit matures early.

'Seneca Gourmet,' 46 days. Medium green fruit with white flecks grows to 8 inches long. *'Super Select,'* 48 days. Upright plant bears dark green fruit with light green flecks. Fruit grows to 8 inches long. Tolerant of downy mildew and powdery mildew. *'Zucchini Elite,'* 48 days. Fruit grows to 8 inches long, and has glossy, dark green skin with pale green flecks. Hybrid. *'Zucchini Select,'* 47 days. Long-stemmed fruit grows to 6 inches in length and has shiny, medium green skin with pale green flecks. Tolerant of downy mildew and powdery mildew. Hybrid.

Growing conditions
Squash can be started from seeds or from purchased seedlings, but neither should be transplanted outdoors until all danger of frost has passed and the soil is warm. Seeds that are sown directly in the soil should be sown ½ inch deep. Seeds can also be started indoors in spring, approximately three weeks before the last frost date, and then moved into the garden. Germination takes 10 days. The seedlings should be thinned to a spacing of 3 feet apart.

Summer squash thrives in hot weather and is heat-resistant.

Soil for squash should be rich, well drained and fertile. Mix 5-10-5 into the soil before planting and fertilize again every three weeks.

Squash plants are susceptible to damage from the squash borer, squash bug, aphid, cucumber beetle, mildew, wilt and damping-off.

Harvesting
The fruit of summer squash is harvested when it is still immature, meaning the skin is still soft and can be pierced with a fingernail. Although squash can be left to grow as large as desired, the flavor of cylindrical types is best when the fruit is about 5 inches long and 1½ to 2 inches in diameter; the flavor of scallop types is best when they are 3 to 4 inches across. Squash grows quickly, and the plant should be checked daily to see if the fruit needs harvesting. Frequent harvesting ensures that the plant will keep producing.

—

Sweet Potato
Ipomoea batatus

The sweet potato is an oblong edible root with flesh that ranges from pale yellow to orange. The plant is a low-growing vine with dark green, pointed leaves on short runners. It produces petunia-like blossoms in early summer. Sweet potatoes are sometimes called yams, but this is a misnomer. The yam is a tropical vegetable of the genus *Dioscorea*.

Selected varieties
'Bush Porto Rico,' 125 days from root cuttings to mature root. Compact plant that takes up less space than other varieties; the vine grows to only 18 inches. Potatoes have copper-colored skins and red-orange flesh. *'Centennial,'* 95 days. Copper-colored skin and orange flesh. Matures faster than other varieties and is the best choice for areas with a short growing season.

Growing conditions
Sweet potatoes are grown from slips—seed potatoes (pieces of potatoes) that have already sprouted and developed roots. Slips should be certified disease-

'ZUCCHINI ELITE' SQUASH

'CENTENNIAL' SWEET POTATO

'FORDHOOK GIANT' SWISS CHARD

'RHUBARB' SWISS CHARD

free by the state agriculture department. The slips can be planted outdoors in spring after all danger of frost has passed and the soil is warm. They should be spaced 15 to 18 inches apart. The bottom of the cutting should be placed 5 to 6 inches deep in the soil; some of the lower leaves on the stem can be buried.

Sweet potatoes are heat-tolerant and drought-resistant. They need a long growing season in which night temperatures will not drop below 60° F. Soil should be well drained, dry, sandy and slightly acid. Fertilize with 5-10-5 prior to planting and do not fertilize again during the season. Too much fertilizer will cause the plant to produce lush foliage instead of full-sized potatoes.

Sweet potatoes are susceptible to damage from aphids, cucumber beetles, flea beetles, leafhoppers and nematodes.

Harvesting

Sweet potatoes are harvested at the time of the first fall frost. All potatoes should be removed from the ground then because frost can damage them.

Dig carefully around the potatoes so their skin is not damaged. Lift them out of the soil and allow them to dry out on the ground for several hours. Keep the potatoes in a warm, humid, dark place for two weeks; then move them to a cool area—approximately 50° F—for storage.

Swiss Chard

Beta vulgaris, Cicla Group

Swiss chard is a relative of the beet. Unlike the beet, it is not grown for its root; it is grown for its edible stems and leaves. The leaves, which have thick midribs and wide veins, can be eaten either raw or cooked. The plant grows from 24 to 28 inches high.

Selected varieties

'Fordhook Giant,' 60 days from seed to mature leaves. Dark green, crumpled leaves are thick and fleshy. Stems are 2½ inches wide and white; leaf veins are also white. Drought-resistant. Does not do well in sandy soil. 'Large White Rib,' 60 days. Broad, flat stems are silvery white; medium green leaves are smooth, thick and tender with white veins. This variety does well in sandy soils.

'Lucullus,' 50 days. Light yellow-green leaves are heavily curled and crumpled; slender stalks are creamy white. 'Rhubarb,' 60 days. Resembles rhubarb with translucent, heavy red stalks and red veins. Leaves are deep green, glossy and heavily crumpled. An attractive plant that is also grown for its ornamental value.

Growing conditions

Swiss chard is grown from seeds sown directly in the soil in early spring, about three weeks before the last spring frost is expected. Seeds should be sown 2 to 3 inches apart and ½ inch deep. Germination takes 10 days.

A chard seed, like a beet seed, is actually a small fruit that contains several seeds. To prevent overcrowding, thinning must be done immediately after germination. Then, when the seedlings are 6 to 8 inches high, thin them again to stand 6 inches apart. The thinnings can be eaten.

Swiss Chard will tolerate poor soil conditions, but for the best growth and flavor, soil should be loose, rich and well drained, and have a pH that is close to neutral. Fertilize prior to planting with 5-10-5, and again every six weeks during the growing season. Swiss chard is one of the most heat-resistant greens.

Although Swiss chard is generally free of insects and diseases, it may be attacked by leaf miners and plant bugs.

Harvesting

Cut off the outer leaves when they are 6 to 8 inches long, and leave the inner leaves to develop for later harvesting. Or cut the entire plant off about 1 inch above the ground; the plant will then produce new leaves, which will be ready for cutting in a few weeks.

—

Tabasco Peppers see Peppers

—

Tampala
Amaranthus tricolor

Tampala is a leafy green vegetable similar to spinach, but unlike spinach, the plant can withstand summer heat. Leaves are heart-shaped, 4 inches long, and green with orange, red or purple tips. The leaves can be used in cooking or in salads. The full-grown plant is bushy and can reach 6 feet tall, but tampala is usually harvested at an immature stage.

Selected varieties
There are no named varieties of tampala; it is sold under its common name. The plant matures in 70 days from seed to ripe leaves.

Growing conditions
Tampala is grown from seed planted directly in the soil in spring, after all danger of frost has passed. The seed should be sown ¼ inch deep and 2 inches apart. Germination takes seven to 10 days. When seedlings are 4 inches tall, they should be thinned to about 6 inches apart. The thinnings can be used in salads and soups. To have a continuous supply of tampala all summer, seeds can be sown every two weeks until one month prior to the first frost date.

Tampala thrives in high heat and is drought-tolerant. Soil should be average and well drained. Before planting, mix 5-10-5 into the soil.

No further fertilizing will be needed during the growing season.

Harvesting
When the plant is 6 to 8 inches high, remove the entire plant by cutting it off at ground level. If tampala is allowed to grow into a large, shrubby plant, only the top 5 inches of the branch tips should be cut for harvest.

—

Tomatillo
Physalis ixocarpa

The tomatillo can add a Mexican touch to cooking. Its pulpy fruit, less watery than the tomato, is often used as a base for salsa. The fruit is round, about 2¼ inches across and resembles a small tomato, but it is green even at maturity. Each fruit forms inside a papery husk that resembles a Chinese lantern. The plant grows to 4 feet tall, with long, deeply notched leaves and yellow flowers.

Selected varieties
There are no named varieties of tomatillo; it is sold under its common name. The plants mature from seed to fruit in 100 days.

Growing conditions
The tomatillo is started from seed. You may purchase seed packets or buy ripe fresh fruit and remove its seeds. Wash all pulp from the seeds and let them dry before planting.

Start seeds indoors, four to six weeks before the last spring frost, and transplant the seedlings outdoors as soon as all frost danger has passed. Space the plants 24 to 30 inches apart.

The tomatillo needs a long, warm growing season. Soil should be rich and well drained. Before planting, incorporate 5-10-5 into the soil; no further feeding should be necessary. The tomatillo is drought-resistant.

Tomatillos are susceptible to damage from mites.

TAMPALA

TOMATILLO

'LONG-KEEPER' STANDARD TOMATO

'BETTER BOY VFN' HYBRID TOMATO

Harvesting

As the fruit matures, the husk changes color, from green to red to purple, and begins to open. When the fruit is completely ripe, it will fall out of the husk onto the ground. It can be picked prior to falling and allowed to mature in a warm, light location indoors.

Tomato

Lycopersicon lycopersicum

The most widely homegrown vegetable is the tomato. The tomato is available in sizes ranging from the ¾-inch cherry tomato to the beefsteak tomato that can grow to 5 inches across. There are more varieties of tomato than of any other vegetable. The fruit can be round, oval, globular, oblate or pear-shaped. Although most tomatoes are red, some varieties are yellow and others are orange.

Tomato plants generally belong to either of two groups: determinate or indeterminate. This grouping is based on the plant's growth habits. The determinate tomato is a bushy plant whose terminal growth develops flowers and fruit. When the plant reaches full size, it stops growing, and all the fruit ripens at the same time. This type of tomato is used for canning, juice and other processing. The indeterminate tomato is a vine that continues to grow, flower and produce fruit until it is killed by frost. This type of fruit is best for slicing and salads. Modern seed breeders have developed a variation on those two, a type called intermediate short internode (abbreviated in seed catalogs as ISI). It combines the traits of the other two; it flowers indefinitely, like the indeterminate tomato, but it grows as a compact bush plant (and as such can be caged but not staked—*(page 60)*.

Many varieties are resistant to certain diseases and insects. The resistance is part of the variety's name and is indicated by the letters *V, F, N* or *T*. These initials stand for the variety's resistance to verticillium wilt, fusarium wilt, nematodes or tobacco mosaic. There are two types of fusarium wilt. Those varieties marked *F* are resistant to one type of the disease and those marked *FF* are resistant to both types.

Standard varieties

'Ace 55 VF,' 80 days from seed to ripe fruit. Determinate. Large fruit on a compact plant. *'Beefsteak,'* 90 days. Indeterminate. Large, round fruit can grow to 1 pound. *'Heinz 1350 VF,'* 75 days. Determinate. Excellent for canning. Tomatoes do not crack. *'Long-Keeper,'* 78 days. Determinate. Light golden to orange-red skin. Not as tasty or juicy as others, but stores well.

'Marglobe Improved VF,' 75 days. Determinate. Medium-sized fruit. *'New Yorker V,'* 60 days. Determinate. Small to medium-sized fruit. Early variety, especially good for areas with a short growing season. *'Roma VF,'* 76 days. Determinate. Deep red, plum-shaped fruit; good for juice and tomato paste. *'Rutgers VF,'* 75 days. Determinate. Medium-sized fruit.

'Tropic VF,' 80 days. Indeterminate. Large fruit. Good for areas with a hot climate.

Hybrid varieties

'Avalanche F,' 77 days from seed to ripe fruit. Indeterminate. Medium-sized fruit. *'Beefmaster VFN,'* 80 days. Indeterminate. Very large, slightly flattened fruit; a hybrid version of *'Beefsteak.'* Resists cracking and splitting. *'Better Boy VFN,'* 72 days. Indeterminate. Large fruit is globe-shaped and bright red. Good in hot climates. *'Better Girl VFN,'* 62 days. Indeterminate. Matures early. Crack-resistant.

'Big Boy,' 78 days. Indeterminate. Large, globe-shaped fruit with strong flavor. *'Big Early,'* 62 days. Indeterminate. Medium-

sized, globe-shaped fruit; not as meaty as *'Better Girl.'* *'Big Girl VF,'* 78 days. Indeterminate. Large fruit with mild, sweet flavor. Crack-resistant. *'Big Pick VFFNT,'* 70 days. Indeterminate. Large, round fruit. One of the most disease-resistant tomatoes.

'Bragger,' 75 days. Indeterminate. One of the largest tomatoes. The fruit has a tendency to crack and split. *'Celebrity VFFNT,'* 70 days. Determinate. Medium-sized, globe-shaped, firm fruit. Similar to *'Floramerica,'* but plant produces more fruit. This variety is a good choice for a garden with limited space. Crack-resistant. *'Champion VFNT,'* 62 days. Indeterminate. Large, sweet fruit. One of the earliest-maturing beefsteak tomatoes.

'Early Girl V,' 54 days. Indeterminate. One of the earliest varieties. Small fruit with slightly flattened shape. Tart and juicy. *'Early Pick VF,'* 62 days. Indeterminate. Early, medium-sized fruit, similar to *'Big Early,'* but is wilt-tolerant. *'Fantastic,'* 65 days. Indeterminate. Medium-sized, globe-shaped fruit matures early. *'Floramerica VFF,'* 75 days. Determinate. Medium-sized scarlet fruit on a compact plant. Especially good in the South and the West; it produces in hot, humid, rainy conditions.

'Heartland VFN,' 68 days. Indeterminate. Medium-sized fruit on a compact plant. *'Lady Luck VFT,'* 78 days. Indeterminate. 78 days. Large fruit similar to *'Big Girl'* and *'Big Boy.'* *'La Roma VFF,'* 62 days. Determinate. Used for making tomato paste; more productive than the older, nonhybrid *'Roma.'* *'Mamma Mia VFF,'* 62 days. Determinate. Meaty, pear-shaped fruit used to make tomato paste. Plant is more productive than other paste types.

'Pink Girl VFT,' 76 days. Indeterminate. Medium-sized fruit has pink skin. Juicy with mild flavor. Crack-resistant. *'Quick Pick VFFNT,'* 60 days. Indeterminate. Very early, medium-sized fruit. Not as meaty as other hybrids. Resistant to *Alternaria.* *'Spring Set VF,'* 65 days. Determinate. Compact plant with early, medium-sized fruit. Good for cold climates.

'Super Fantastic VFN,' 70 days. Indeterminate. Large, meaty fruit. Does well even in poor soil conditions. *'Supersteak VFN,'* 80 days. Indeterminate. Exceptionally large, slightly flattened fruit, which can grow to 1 pound or more. Very rich flavor. Smoothest beefsteak-type fruit. *'The Juice VF,'* 65 days. Determinate. Rich flavor. Good for canning and juice. *'Whopper VFNT,'* 70 days. Indeterminate. Extremely large, juicy, meaty fruit.

Cherry varieties
'Gardeners Delight,' 65 days from seed to ripe fruit. Indeterminate. Very sweet, bright red tomatoes in clusters of six to 12 fruits. Nonhybrid. *'Red Cherry,'* 72 days. Indeterminate. Scarlet fruit 1 inch across grows in clusters. Nonhybrid. *'Sweet 100,'* 68 days. Indeterminate. Extremely sweet cherry tomato produced in long, heavy clusters of 100 fruits. One of the earliest to mature. Very high in vitamin C content. Hybrid.

Yellow-fruited varieties
'Golden Boy,' 80 days from seed to ripe fruit. Indeterminate. Mild flavor; low in acid. Bright yellow, medium-sized, globe-shaped fruit. Hybrid. *'Jubilee,'* Indeterminate. 75 days. Golden orange fruit with milder flavor than most red tomatoes. Nonhybrid. *'Lemon Boy VFN,'* 72 days. Indeterminate. Medium-sized fruit; more flavorful than other yellow varieties. Hybrid.

'Sunray,' 80 days. Determinate. Yellow-orange skin and flesh. Large, globe-shaped fruit with mild flavor. Nonhybrid. *'Yellow Pear,'* 70 days. Indeterminate. Pear-shaped yellow tomato with mild fla-

'LA ROMA VFF' HYBRID TOMATO

'SWEET 100' CHERRY TOMATO

'LEMON BOY VFN' YELLOW-FRUITED TOMATO

'YELLOW PLUM' TOMATO

'TINY TIM' CONTAINER TOMATO

vor. Nonhybrid. *'Yellow Plum,'* Indeterminate. Plum-shaped. Best yellow variety for cooking and preserving. Nonhybrid.

Container varieties

'Basket King,' 55 days from seed to ripe fruit. Determinate. Very early, sweet cherry tomatoes for containers or baskets. Hybrid. *'Better Bush VFN,'* 72 days. ISI. Large, juicy, meaty fruit on a very compact plant. *'Florida Basket,'* 70 days. Determinate. Ideal for hanging baskets. Nonhybrid. *'Patio,'* 70 days. Determinate. Medium-sized fruit. May need staking. Hybrid.

'Pixie,' 52 days. Determinate. Ripens faster than other cherry tomatoes. Upright, stocky plants. Can be grown indoors. Hybrid. *'Super Bush VFN,'* 80 days. Determinate. Small to medium-sized, meaty fruit on a very compact plant that requires no staking. Excellent for small gardens and containers. *'Tiny Tim,'* 55 days. Determinate. Plant grows to only 15 inches tall and produces ¾-inch cherry tomatoes. Nonhybrid.

Growing conditions

Tomatoes are grown from seeds or purchased plants. Seeds should be started indoors because the germination rate is much higher than it would be if they were planted directly in the soil. Seeds can be started from six to eight weeks before the last frost date. Germination takes six to 10 days. Seedlings can be transplanted into the garden or into individual containers after all danger of frost has passed and nights are above 60° F. The plants should be set into the soil deeper than they grew in the pot or flat so roots will form along the stem and produce a stronger plant.

The spacing of plants depends on the type of tomato and the manner of support. Planting distance should be 24 inches for determinate or ISI tomatoes, which should not be staked. Indeterminate tomatoes that are staked should be spaced 18 inches apart, and indeterminate tomatoes that are caged *(page 60)* should be spaced 30 to 36 inches apart. Indeterminate tomatoes that are not staked or caged should be spaced 40 to 48 inches apart.

Although indeterminate tomatoes can be allowed to grow on the ground and will produce twice as much fruit as indeterminate tomatoes that are supported, the supported plants produce larger tomatoes that ripen faster.

Soil for tomatoes should be evenly moist, well drained, with a pH of 5.5 to 7.0 and high in organic matter. Fertilize before planting and then once a month until harvest. Mulch should be applied after planting to keep the soil evenly moist and prevent blossom-end rot. The plants should not be watered just prior to harvesting; watering at this time would cause the fruit to crack and acquire a bland, watery taste.

Fruit production will decrease if the soil becomes cool, during periods of heavy rain and when there are hot, dry winds. Plant leaves may curl up, especially in hot weather. This is a normal occurrence and does not affect the plant's production.

Tomatoes can be damaged by aphids, whiteflies, Colorado potato beetles, leafhoppers, cutworms, tomato hornworms, spider mites, slugs, nematodes, blight and blossom-end rot.

Harvesting

Tomatoes can be picked from the plant as they ripen. Just prior to the first fall frost, pick all of the remaining full-sized tomatoes and ripen them indoors. To ripen, the fruit needs two weeks at a temperature of 70° F and another four weeks at 55° F. The tomatoes can be ripened on a windowsill out of direct sunlight and then stored in the refrigerator.

Watercress
Nasturtium officinale

Watercress is an aquatic plant that needs a moist environment. Each plant grows to 4 inches tall and spreads into a mat about 12 inches across. The plant has small, thin, round green leaves; it blooms in spring, producing tiny, pale flowers that resemble nasturtiums. Watercress is grown for its pungent, peppery-tasting foliage, which can be used in salads or as a garnish. It is a perennial in areas with winter temperatures as low as − 10° F; in areas with colder temperatures, it must be replanted each spring.

Selected varieties
There are no named varieties of watercress; it is sold under its common name. Plants mature in 60 days from seed to ripe leaves.

Growing conditions
Watercress can be grown from seed or from started plants, which can be purchased at a nursery or a grocery store. Seeds are started indoors in early spring and should be kept out of direct sunlight in a cool area where the temperature does not exceed 55° F. The planting medium must be light and constantly moist; the seeds should not be covered. Germination takes seven to 10 days.

Seeds or started plants may also be planted outdoors in early spring. They can be sown in a sandy garden bed or in water, in a garden pond or a stream. The plants should be set 8 to 12 inches apart. Seedlings started in a stream or other source of running water can be held in place with small stones or pebbles at the base of their stems until the roots take hold.

Watercress can tolerate full sun if it is grown in water. If it is in soil, it needs partial shade, or heat and dryness will cause the leaves to acquire a bitter taste.

Soil should be fertile, sandy and well drained, with a pH of 7.0. The roots require a constant supply of moisture, so plants should be watered every day. Watercress can become invasive, and may need to be pruned or thinned each spring.

Watercress is insect- and disease-free.

Harvesting
Stems may be cut after the plant has bloomed. If the tops are snipped off, the plants will continue producing for harvest throughout the summer until the first frost. Watercress should not be harvested while the plants are in bloom, because the leaves will have a strong, slightly bitter taste then.

—

Winter Squash
Cucurbita

Although they are grown in the summer, these members of the squash family are called winter squash because they store well after the fall harvest and into the winter months.

Winter squash are vining plants. The fruit is eaten when it matures, meaning when the rind or skin becomes hard. Only the flesh is edible. The vine grows to 8 inches high and sprawls along the ground for several feet.

There are several types of winter squash and they are members of different *Cucurbita* species. Acorn and spaghetti squash are *C. pepo*; butternut squash is *C. moschata*; Hubbard and turban squash are *C. maxima*.

Acorn varieties produce dark green, sometimes orange-streaked fruit that is round and deeply ribbed and resembles a large acorn. Butternut varieties are shaped like large pears and have long, thick, cylindrical necks. Hubbard varieties are rounded fruits with ribbed, bumpy skin that is dark green, gold or blue-gray. Turban squash has a flattened shape with a thick, round center resembling a crown or a tur-

WATERCRESS

'JERSEY GOLDEN' ACORN SQUASH

'TABLE ACE' ACORN SQUASH

'BUTTER BOY' BUTTERNUT SQUASH

'BLUE HUBBARD' SQUASH

'SPAGHETTI' SQUASH

ban. Spaghetti squash is round or oblong with yellow skin and stringy yellow-orange flesh.

The squash varieties listed below are nonhybrids unless otherwise indicated.

Acorn varieties

'Autumn Queen,' 71 days from seed to ripe fruit. Semibush plant. Fruit has dark green skin with bright orange flesh that is less stringy than other acorn varieties. *'Early Acorn,'* 75 days. Semibush type, compact plant. Orange-yellow flesh with smooth texture. Hybrid. *'Jersey Golden,'* 60-80 days. Can be harvested early like summer squash or eaten as winter squash. Flesh is light yellow to light orange; skin is golden. Ideal for small gardens. *'Royal Acorn,'* 90 days. One of the larger acorn varieties; the fruit can grow to 8 inches in diameter. Dark green skin with orange flesh.

'Table Ace,' 70 days. Semibush plant with black shell and fiberless bright orange flesh. Earlier than *'Table King.'* Hybrid. *'Table King,'* 75 days. Glossy, smooth, dark green shell and thick golden flesh. *'Table Queen,'* 90 days. Semibush plant. Fruit has dark green skin, orange flesh and grows to 8 inches in diameter. Strong, nutty flavor.

Butternut varieties

'Burpee's Butterbush,' 75 days from seed to ripe fruit. Compact, bushy vine grows to only 3 feet long. Fruit has orange skin and deep orange flesh. *'Butter Boy,'* 80 days. Extra sweet, nutty flavor from reddish orange flesh. Relatively compact plant. Hybrid.

'Early Butternut Hybrid,' 80 days. Compact vine. Fruit has thin, tan skin and orange flesh. Stores well. *'Waltham,'* 85 days. Flesh is solid, dry and light; rind is dark orange to tan. Relatively large plant. *'Zenith Hybrid,'* 88 days. The fruit is slightly smaller than *'Waltham,'* but similar in shape. The vine is also

smaller than *'Waltham,'* but yields more fruit per plant.

Hubbard varieties

'Blue Hubbard,' 120 days from seed to ripe fruit. Blue-gray, slightly ridged fruit with fine, sweet, bright yellow-orange flesh. *'Golden Hubbard,'* 90 days. Skin is orange-red with medium-sized warts. Flesh is dark orange. *'Hubbard Improved Green,'* 120 days. Dark green skin is lightly warted; flesh is orange. Fruit can grow to 10 pounds. *'True Hubbard,'* 115 days. Dark bronze-green skin with sweet, fine, yellow-orange flesh. Smaller than *'Blue Hubbard.'*

'Warted Hubbard,' 110 days. Skin is dark green, rough and heavily warted. The orange flesh is smooth and less stringy than other Hubbard varieties. Stores well.

Spaghetti varieties

'Spaghetti,' 100 days from seed to ripe fruit. Also called vegetable spaghetti. Flesh looks like light golden spaghetti when cooked and can be used as a substitute for pasta. Fruit is large and oval with a light yellow skin.

Turban varieties

'Buttercup,' 105 days from seed to ripe fruit. Thick orange flesh that tastes like sweet potato. Its skin is dark green with silvery stripes and gray spots. The fruit is squat and cylindrical. *'Turk's Turban,'* 105 days. Bright orange or red fruit with white or green stripes grows to 10 inches across. Fruit is in a flattened, turban-hat shape.

Growing conditions

Squash can be started from seeds or from purchased seedlings, but neither should be planted outdoors until all danger of frost has passed and the soil is warm. Seeds sown directly in the soil should be sown ½ inch deep. Seeds can also be started indoors in spring, about three weeks before the last frost date, and then moved into the garden. Germination takes 10 days. The seedlings should be thinned to a spacing of about 4 feet apart.

Soil for squash should be rich, well drained and fertile. Mix 5-10-5 into the soil before planting and fertilize again every three weeks.

Squash plants are susceptible to damage from the squash borer, squash bug, aphid, cucumber beetle, mildew, wilt and damping-off.

Harvesting.
Winter squash is cut from the vine when the rind becomes hard. Leave a part of the stem on the squash to prevent its rotting during storage.

—

Zucchini see Summer Squash

'TURK'S TURBAN' SQUASH

FURTHER READING

American Horticultural Society, *Vegetables.* Mount Vernon, Virginia: American Horticultural Society, 1980.

Bailey, Liberty Hyde, and Ethel Zoe Bailey, *Hortus Third: A Concise Dictionary of Plants Cultivated in the United States and Canada.* New York: Macmillan, 1976.

Ball, Jeff, *The Self-Sufficient Suburban Garden.* Emmaus, Pennsylvania: Rodale Press, 1983.

Bartholomew, Mel, *Square Foot Gardening.* Emmaus, Pennsylvania: Rodale Press, 1981.

Baumgardt, John Philip, *The Practical Vegetable Gardener.* New York: Quick Fox, 1978.

Bush-Brown, James, and Louise Bush-Brown, *America's Garden Book.* New York: Charles Scribner's Sons, 1980.

Carleton, R. Milton, *The New Vegetable and Fruit Gardening Book.* Chicago: Contemporary Books, 1976.

Creasy, Rosalind, *The Complete Book of Edible Landscaping.* San Francisco: Sierra Club, 1982.

Crockett, James Underwood, *Crockett's Victory Garden.* Boston: Little, Brown, 1977.

Dietz, Marjorie J., ed., *10,000 Garden Questions Answered by 20 Experts.* Garden City, New York: Doubleday, 1982.

Doty, Walter L., *All about Vegetables.* San Francisco: Ortho Books/Chevron Chemical Company, 1981.

Fell, Derek, *Vegetables: How to Select, Grow and Enjoy.* Tucson, Arizona: HP Books, 1982.

Hunt, Marjorie B., and Brenda Bortz, *High-Yield Gardening.* Emmaus, Pennsylvania: Rodale Press, 1986.

Lammers, Susan M., ed., *All about Tomatoes.* San Francisco: Ortho Books/Chevron Chemical Company, 1981.

Larkcom, Joy, *The Salad Garden.* New York: Viking Press, 1984.

MacCaskey, Michael, ed., *Complete Guide to Basic Gardening.* Tucson, Arizona: HP Books, 1986.

Organic Gardening magazine, *The Encyclopedia of Organic Gardening.* Emmaus, Pennsylvania: Rodale Press, 1978.

Poincelot, Raymond P., *No-Dig, No-Weed Gardening.* Emmaus, Pennsylvania: Rodale Press, 1986.

Reilly, Ann, *Success with Seeds.* Greenwood, South Carolina: George W. Park Seed Company, 1978.

Schuler, Stanley, *Gardens Are for Eating.* New York: Macmillan, 1975.

Seymour, John, *The Self-Sufficient Gardener: A Complete Guide to Growing and Preserving All Your Own Food.* Garden City, New York: Doubleday, 1978.

Sherf, Arden S., and Arthur Muka, *Insects and Diseases in the Home Vegetable Garden.* Ithaca, New York: New York Cooperative Extension Service, Cornell University, 1978.

Taylor, Norman, *Taylor's Guide to Vegetables & Herbs.* Boston: Houghton Mifflin, 1987.

United States Department of Agriculture, *Gardening for Food and Fun.* Washington, D.C.: United States Department of Agriculture, 1977.

Wyman, Donald, *Wyman's Gardening Encyclopedia.* New York: Macmillan, 1986.

PICTURE CREDITS

The sources for the illustrations in this book are listed below. Cover photograph by Derek Fell. Watercolor paintings by Nicholas Fasciano except pages 8, 9, 11: Sanford Kossin. 86, 87, 88, 89, 90, 91: Lorraine Moseley Epstein. Maps on pages 80, 81, 83, 85: digitized by Richard Furno, inked by John Drummond.

Frontispiece paintings listed by page number: 6: *Spring in Town* by Grant Wood, courtesy The Sheldon Swope Art Gallery, Terre Haute, Indiana. 22: *The Artist's Garden at Eragny* by Camille Pissarro, courtesy National Gallery of Art, Washington, D.C.; Ailsa Mellon Bruce Collection. 50: *Farm Women at Work* by Georges Seurat, courtesy Solomon R. Guggenheim Museum, New York. Photography by Carmelo Guadagno. 66: *Pumpkin Patch* by Winslow Homer, courtesy Mead Art Museum, Amherst College; Museum Purchase 1948.30.

Photographs in Chapters 1 through 4 from the following sources, listed by page number: 8: Larry Lefever/Grant Heilman Photography. 10, 12: © Walter Chandoha 1988. 14: Grant Heilman Photography. 18, 20: © Walter Chandoha 1988. 24, 26: Bob Grant. 28: Derek Fell. 30: Bob Grant. 32: William D. Adams. 36: Grant Heilman Photography. 38, 40: © Walter Chandoha 1988. 44: Horticultural Photography, Corvallis OR. 46: Jerry Howard/Photo-Nats. 48: Thomas Eltzroth. 52: © Walter Chandoha 1988. 54: Bob Grant. 56, 60: Thomas Eltzroth. 64: Runk/Schoenberger/Grant Heilman Photography. 68: Thomas Eltzroth. 70: Horticultural Photography, Corvallis OR. 72: Bob Grant. 74: © Walter Chandoha 1988.

Photographs in the Dictionary of Summer Vegetables are listed by page and numbered from top to bottom. Page 94, 1, 95, 1: Thomas Eltzroth. 96, 1: © Walter Chandoha 1988. 96, 2, 97, 1: Joanne Pavia. 97, 2, 98, 1: Derek Fell. 98, 2: © Walter Chandoha 1988. 99, 1: Derek Fell. 100, 1, 2, 101, 1: Thomas Eltzroth. 101, 2: All America Selections/National Garden Bureau Inc. 102, 1: Ann Reilly. 102, 2: Derek Fell. 103, 1: Thomas Eltzroth. 103, 2: © Northrup King Co. 1988. 104, 1: Grant Heilman Photography. 105, 1: Ann Reilly. 106, 1: William Isom. 106, 2, 107, 1: © Walter Chandoha 1988. 107, 2: Derek Fell. 108, 1: © Walter Chandoha 1988. 108, 2: Thomas Eltzroth. 109, 1: William D. Adams. 110, 1, 2: © Walter Chandoha 1988. 110, 3: Derek Fell. 111, 1: Ann Reilly. 111, 2: Derek Fell. 111, 3: © Walter Chandoha 1988. 112, 1, 113, 1: Thomas Eltzroth. 114, 1, 2: Derek Fell. 114, 3: Dr. Gilbert McCollum. 115, 1: © Walter Chandoha 1988. 115, 2: Ann Reilly. 116, 1, 3: Thomas Eltzroth. 116, 2: Derek Fell. 117, 1, 2: Thomas Eltzroth. 117, 3: © Walter Chandoha 1988. 118, 1: Derek Fell. 119, 1: Thomas Eltzroth. 120, 1: © Walter Chandoha 1988. 121, 1: Thomas Eltzroth. 121, 2: Horticultural Photography, Corvallis OR. 122, 1: Derek Fell. 122, 2, 123, 1, 2: © Walter Chandoha 1988. 124, 1: Derek Fell. 124, 2: Thomas Eltzroth. 25, 1: Derek Fell. 125, 2: Ann Reilly. 126, 1: Derek Fell. 126, 2: Ann Reilly. 126, 3: Derek Fell. 127, 1: Ivan Massar/Photo-Nats. 127, 2: Thomas Eltzroth. 128, 1, 2: Ann Reilly. 129, 1, 2: Derek Fell. 130, 1, 2: Derek Fell. 131, 1, 3: Ann Reilly. 131, 2: © Walter Chandoha 1988. 132, 1: Thomas Eltzroth. 132, 2: © Walter Chandoha 1988. 133, 1: Ann Reilly. 133, 2, 3: Derek Fell. 134, 1: William D. Adams. 134, 2: John Smith/Photo-Nats. 134, 3: Derek Fell. 135, 1: Thomas Eltzroth.

ACKNOWLEDGMENTS

The index for this book was prepared by Lynne R. Hobbs. The editors also wish to thank: David Anderson, George W. Park Seed Company, Greenwood, South Carolina; Anna Caroline Ball, Ball Seed Company, Rochester, New York; Dr. Thomas H. Barksdale, U.S.D.A. Horticultural Science Institute, Beltsville, Maryland; Robert Bennett, Bala Cynwyd, Pennsylvania; Sarah Brash, Alexandria, Virginia; Sarah Broley, Washington, D.C.; Michael Dupree, Alexandria Extension Service, Alexandria, Virginia; Carol M. Eichner, U.S.D.A. Horticultural Science Institute, Beltsville, Maryland; Betsy Frankel, Alexandria, Virginia; Cathy Green, Economic Research Service, Washington, D.C.; Kenneth E. Hancock, Annandale, Virginia; Paul Ledig, Petoseed Company, Saticoy, California; Jim McFearson, Petoseed Research Station, Bridgeton, New Jersey; William J. Park, George W. Park Seed Company, Greenwood, South Carolina; Jayne E. Rohrich, Alexandria, Virginia; Joseph Savage, Nassau County Cooperative Extension Service, Plainview, New York; Cristina Schwartz, Washington, D.C.; Candace H. Scott, College Park, Maryland; Marilyn M. Terrell, Annandale, Virginia; Mel Tessene, Harris Moran Seed Company, Rochester, New York; Barbara Tufty, Washington, D.C.; Jan Unstead, Ball Seed Company, West Chicago, Illinois; Richard Weir, Nassau County Cooperative Extension Service, Plainview, New York; Richard and Corinne Willard, Comstock, Ferre & Co., Wethersfield, Connecticut; Susan Zidal, Arlington, Virginia.

INDEX

REDEFINITION

Senior Editors	Anne Horan, Robert G. Mason
Design Director	Robert Barkin
Designer	Edwina Smith
Illustration	Nicholas Fasciano
Design Assistant	Sue Pratt
Pictures	Deborah Thornton
Production Editor	Anthony K. Pordes
Research	Gail Prensky, Barbara B. Smith, Mary Yee
Text Editor	Sharon Cygan
Writers	Gerald Jonas, Ann Reilly, David S. Thomson
Business Manager	Catherine M. Chase
PRESIDENT	Edward Brash

THE CONSULTANTS

C. Colston Burrell is the general consultant for The Time-Life Gardener's Guide. He is Curator of Plant Collections at the Minnesota Landscape Arboretum, part of the University of Minnesota, where he oversees plant collections and develops regional interest in the horticulture of the upper Midwest. Mr. Burrell is the author of publications about ferns and wildflowers, and a former curator of Native Plant Collections at the National Arboretum in Washington, D.C.

Wayne Ambler, consultant for *Summer Vegetables,* is a horticulturist in Richmond, Virginia. He is a member of the adjunct faculty at J. Sargeant Reynolds Community College and at Patrick Henry High School in Ashland, Virginia, where he teaches horticulture.

Library of Congress Cataloging-in-Publication Data
Summer vegetables.
    p. cm.—(The Time-Life gardener's guide)
    Bibliograpy: p.
    Includes index.
    1. Vegetable gardening. 2. Vegetables.
I. Time-Life Books. II. Series.
SB321.S85 1988   635—dc19   88-1153 CIP
ISBN 0-8094-6608-2
ISBN 0-8094-6609-0 (lib. bdg.)